THE DCC GUIDE

— SECOND EDITION —

Don Fiehmann

KALMBACH BOOKS

Preface

When I first started to write articles back in the 1960s I advanced to an IBM electric typewriter. In the '70s, the typewriter was replaced with a new IBM "golfball" (Selectric) typewriter. That typewriter was later modified and connected to a Heathkit computer. In the '90s I stepped up to an IBM PC, which was eventually replaced with IBM laptop. After the start of the new century I got an iPad. Soon after, I gave the iPad to my wife to read books and I obtained an iPad 4 with camera and voice-to-text feature.

Model railroading has also benefited as technology has advanced. DCC continues to improve. The Internet has brought modelers from all over the world closer. New sound files can be updated over the Internet. Locomotives and layouts can be operated with a smartphones via Wi-Fi using Java Model Railroad Interface. It all makes one wonder what is going to happen to the hobby in the next few years...

— *Don Fiehmann*

Kalmbach Books
21027 Crossroads Circle
Waukesha, Wisconsin 53186
www.Kalmbach.com/Books

Published in 2014
18 17 16 15 14   1 2 3 4 5

Manufactured in China

ISBN: 978-1-62700-103-8
EISBN: 978-1-62700-104-5

Editor: Jeff Wilson
Art Director: Tom Ford

Unless otherwise noted, all photographs were taken by the author.

Publisher's Cataloging-In-Publication Data

Fiehmann, Don, author.
  The DCC guide / Don Fiehmann. -- Second edition.

    pages : color illustrations ; cm. -- (Model railroader books) -- (Wiring & electronics)

  Issued also as an ebook.
  ISBN: 978-1-62700-103-8

  1. Digital control systems. 2. Railroads--Models--Electronic equipment. 3. Railroads--Models--Design and construction. I. Title. II. Series: Model railroader books.

TF197 .F54 2014
625.1/9

Contents

Chapter 1
DCC evolution 4

Chapter 2
DCC components .8

Chapter 3
Basic DCC technology 11

Chapter 4
Basics of decoders 15

Chapter 5
Decoder programming 22

Chapter 6
How to choose a DCC system 33

Chapter 7
Wiring a layout for DCC 41

Chapter 8
Decoder installation 52

Chapter 9
Using LEDs and bulbs with DCC 62

Chapter 10
Installing speakers and sound decoders 68

Chapter 11
Operating with DCC 75

Chapter 12
DCC and today's technology 81

Glossary of DCC terms 85

Troubleshooting 86

DCC manufacturers and suppliers 87

Acknowledgements 87

CHAPTER ONE

DCC evolution

Digital Command Control systems allow operators to control their trains independently without regard for electrical blocks. Most systems, such as EasyDCC from CVP Products—shown here on *Model Railroader* magazine's HO scale Milwaukee, Racine & Troy club layout—allow the option of wireless radio control. *Jim Forbes*

Over the years, improvements in technology have increased the quality of model railroad operations. Direct-current (DC) power packs became transistorized, walkaround control became practical, and locomotive motors improved significantly. The latest improvement is Digital Command Control (DCC). Representing a major change from standard DC control, DCC allows operators to run their trains independently of other trains without regard to switching electrical blocks.

Early systems

General Electric's Astrac, introduced in the early 1960s, is the grandfather of command-control systems. With Astrac, no longer did you have to fiddle with a bunch of toggle switches to run your train around the layout. Instead, receivers installed in locomotives responded to signals sent through the rails, **1**.

Astrac was an analog system with control channels for five locomotives. It was a state-of-the-art system in the 1960s, using discrete solid-state parts. Expansion to additional channels was planned, but GE discontinued the system before this happened. Although short-lived, operationally limited, and expensive, Astrac was important in giving model railroaders a taste of the future of locomotive and layout control.

Other command-control systems eventually appeared, including CTC-16, CTC-80, Dynatrol, and Onboard. In the 1980s, the Onboard system offered a new dimension to command control: sound! These newer systems packed more functions into smaller receivers by using integrated circuits (ICs), **2**.

Early analog systems suffered from a combination of problems, including operational malfunctions due to heat, a limited number of channels (addresses), and a reliance on proprietary components.

The modular model railroading group I worked with in the 1980s used an analog system. When running the layout at shows, operators would often lose control of their locomotives in the afternoon after they had operated for a long time. When the engines were turned off and allowed to cool, they were okay. These heat-related problems disappeared when the group switched to DCC.

Analog systems offered a limited number of addresses, and it was a hassle to keep track of which channel number matched which locomotive. Digital Command Control fixed this with a range of 9,999 addresses, allowing the locomotive's cab number to be the decoder's address.

A lack of standards also plagued analog systems. Each system was

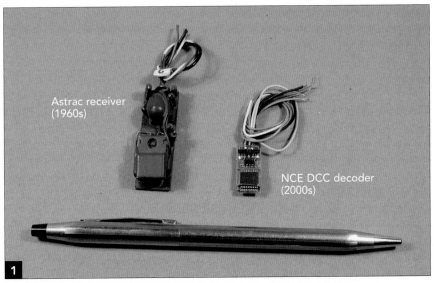

1 Compare the pioneering Astrac receiver (which was available with five pre-set addresses) at left to the much smaller NCE DCC decoder, which can be programmed with more than 10,000 addresses and control forward and reverse lights.

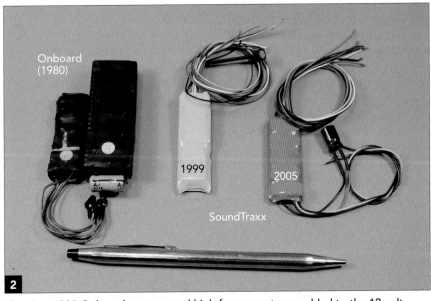

2 The circa-1980 Onboard system used high-frequency tones added to the 12-volt track power for control and selection. The Onboard receiver has two parts: one for control and the other for sound. In the late 1990s, SoundTraxx introduced its line of DCC sound decoders. The device at right is the Tsunami 16-bit sound decoder.

different, with no cross-compatibility. If you bought a system and needed to expand it, there was only one source for components. If a manufacturer went out of business, you were out of luck unless you could find used equipment of the same brand.

Developing a standard

The National Model Railroad Association (NMRA) realized the need for a standardized command control system. In the 1980s the organization

began looking for a solution. A basic method of combining power and data on the rails was needed, and the approach that looked most promising was a digital system developed by Berndt Lenz. The NMRA obtained permission to use the Lenz digital method, leading to the NMRA releasing its DCC specifications in the mid-1990s.

The NMRA divides its specifications into two basic parts: standards (indicated by an S prefix) and

3 NMRA Standards and Recommended Practices	
Standard S-9.1	DCC electrical standard
Standard S-9.2	DCC communications standard
Recommended Practice RP-9.1.1	DCC electrical interface and wire color code
Recommended Practice RP-9.1.2	DCC power station interface
Recommended Practice RP-9.2.1	DCC extended-packet format
Recommended Practice RP-9.2.2	DCC configuration variables (CVs)
RP-9.2.2 Appendix A	Manufacturers' ID codes
Recommended Practice RP-9.2.3	DCC service mode
Recommended Practice RP-9.2.4	DCC fail-safe
Recommended Practice RP-9.3.1	DCC electrical specification for decoder transmission
Recommended Practice RP-9.3.2	DCC basic decoder transmission

Most Digital Command Control-related items bear the NMRA's logo for DCC.

recommended practices (RP prefix), 3. More detailed information on S-9 and RP-9 can be found online at www.nmra.org.

Technology has evolved in the years since the NMRA first released its DCC specifications, and the model railroad industry has responded with many improvements. The number of decoder configuration variables (CVs) has increased, along with the ability of decoders to handle more functions. Fortunately, many of these advancements fall in the area of recommended practices and not standards. The NMRA has a DCC working group to resolve problems among manufacturers and to suggest changes and improvements.

For example, the initial DCC specifications had only 127 locomotive addresses and 14 speed steps. This was later changed to 9,999 addresses and 28 speed steps. Improved locomotive consisting was added. The latest release added bidirectional data transmission as an option. The requirement for compatibility with 14 speed steps is to

be dropped since all systems now use 28 or 128 speed steps. Turnout control and signaling are also possible with DCC commands.

Digital Command Control has also allowed personal computers to play a big part in model railroad operation. A number of programs enable PCs or Macs to program decoders in locomotives and operate turnouts. Using a computer interface with a DCC system, a dispatcher can sit at a computer and dispatch the railroad using Centralized Traffic Control (CTC). Additional DCC developments have further enhanced the marriage of computers and layouts. The free program JMRI (Java Model Railroad Interface) has gone a long way to make this possible. (See chapter 12).

Without the NMRA, there would be no DCC, as without these standards, we wouldn't have the ability to select items from different manufacturers and have those all work together. Items that pertain to DCC often feature the NMRA's logo for the technology, 4.

Compatibility between brands

Newer DCC equipment from one manufacturer is designed to be compatible with older equipment from another manufacturer. Even with improvements and changes in DCC specifications, components remain compatible.

The DCC standards and recommended practices mainly relate to where the power and digital signal meet on the rails. Consider how television sets are produced: No one tells the manufacturer how to build a TV set or the TV transmitter. But the transmitted signal between the two is controlled by the Federal Communications Commission.

Similarly, the DCC system that puts power and data on the rails is up to the manufacturer. However, the power and data it produces must comply with the NMRA's DCC standards and recommended practices. Each decoder, regardless of manufacturer, must respond correctly to the power and signals on the rails. Examples include SoundTraxx and TCS, two firms that only produce decoders, not systems. Their decoders must be compatible with any DCC system. This is called interoperability.

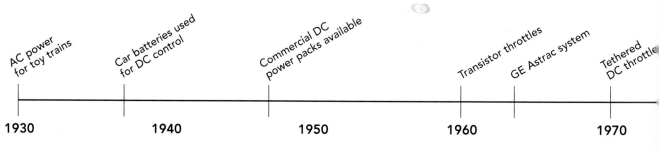

This timeline shows the evolution of model railroad control systems from the 1930s to the present day.

5

These models on Don Fiehmann's layout feature many of the latest DCC technologies. The station lights are controlled by DCC stationary decoders, the illuminated passenger cars and caboose use super capacitors for flicker-free lighting, and the steam locomotive has a SoundTraxx Tsunami sound decoder.

DCC today

In recent years, DCC has gone from being an exception to an expectation, **5.** Even though companies still offer DC locomotives, most are equipped with an 8-, 9-, or 21-pin plug for installing a DCC decoder. As the number of ready-to-run products increases, the hobby's focus is shifting from builders to operators. Digital Command Control has made it easier for a person to visit a layout and run trains without much explanation.

The trend to go wireless seems to be everywhere, including model railroading. While stationary and transistor power packs and tethered walkaround throttles have been a part of the hobby for years, most DCC manufacturers now produce a wireless cabs (throttles) for use with their system. This technology allows operators to follow their trains and control turnouts without being connected to a plug port.

In some cases, technology that we use in our day-to-day lives is being incorporated into model railroading. Lenz uses an adapter (XPA) that allows use of a standard wireless telephone as a cab. If you have a computer with JMRI connected to your DCC system, you can use a smartphone or tablet to run trains via a Wi-Fi connection.

What is the next big frontier for DCC and model railroading? I see a glimmer of light (pun intended) to be television cameras in locomotives, more signaling, layout sounds, and lighting. Super capacitors, which keep trains running over dirty track, are currently add-ons. In the future these will become standard equipment on off-the-shelf models. There is certainly a lot to be excited about.

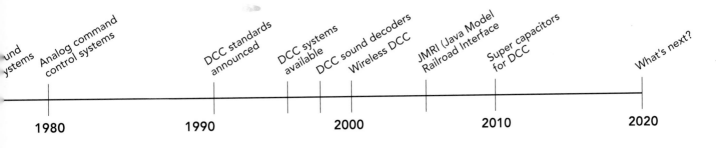

...und systems   Analog command control systems   DCC standards announced   DCC systems available   DCC sound decoders   Wireless DCC   JMRI (Java Model Railroad Interface   Super capacitors for DCC   What's next?

1980   1990   2000   2010   2020

CHAPTER TWO

DCC components

Parts of a DCC system include cabs (throttles), decoders, command stations, boosters, and power supplies. Here's a wireless cab from CVP, a tethered cab from NCE, decoders from Digitrax and Train Control Systems, and an MRC system including tethered cab, combination command station/booster, and power supply.

Digital Command Control systems allow an operator to issue many types of commands, regulating a locomotive's speed and direction as well as controlling lights, sound, and accessories such as turnouts.

The commands travel a path through a number of devices before arriving at the locomotive or accessory decoder. The NMRA's DCC standards apply to the data and power on the rails. The system that generates the DCC signal is up to each manufacturer to design. This means there are many variations on the theme, but mobile and accessory decoders from any manufacturer must follow the NMRA DCC standard to work with all DCC systems. Let's look at the parts that make up a DCC system.

Basic DCC systems

Digital Command Control system operations start with a throttle (cab) which the operator uses to enter instructions, or commands. A system can have multiple cabs. These cabs feed commands to the command station via a cable or wireless connection using radio wireless or infrared (IR) signals.

Each DCC system has one command station, which acts as the brains of the system. The command station generates the data that's sent to the power boosters, **1**. A command station drives one or more boosters. The boosters add power to the data from the command station, then deliver the power and packets of data to the rails.

Decoders take the power and data signal from the rails and analyze the information in the packets (see Chapter 3). A DCC system can have many decoders. Mobile decoders are used in locomotives; accessory (stationary) decoders are used for trackside devices like turnouts and signals, **2**.

Getting commands to the rails

Operation starts with the push of a button or twist of a knob on a cab. The cab (throttle) sends many types of commands, including address selection, speed, and function control to the command station.

The command station serves as the central control for the entire DCC system, gathering data from all of the cabs (and computer if attached). The command station then assembles the commands from the cabs into packets.

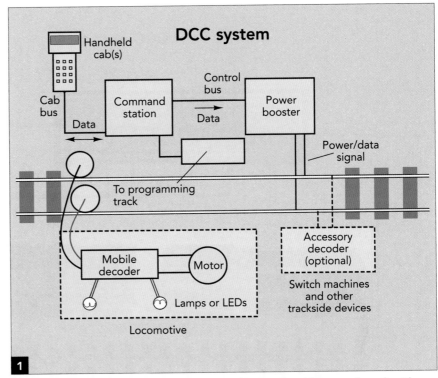

Digital Command Control operations start with a command from a cab or throttle. Signals from the cabs go to the command station, which assembles information from the cabs into packets. The command station sends packets to the booster, which adds the power and then sends the power and packet signal to the rails. The decoder then disassembles the packet and executes the command.

The commands are sorted, prioritized, and then sent to the power booster at a rate of 20 to 150 commands per second. Because wheel/rail contact is often poor, each individual packet is sent a number of times to be sure at least one message gets through to the addressed decoder. When the command station has no packets to send, it fills the time with idle packets. These packets continue supplying power to the rails, but contain no control information.

Once the power booster receives the data packets from the command station, the booster adds power to each packet, and then sends the combined power/data signal to the rails.

Boosters come in a variety of power capacities, and a DCC system can have more than one booster. Each section of a layout fed by a separate booster is called a booster district. Circuit breakers may be used between the boosters and the rails to further divide these districts. Each of these smaller divisions supplied by a circuit breaker is called a power district.

Decoders

Decoders receive the combined power/data signal from the rails, then separate the power from the data signals. Mobile decoders and accessory decoders use separate addresses and packet definitions to ensure command separation and independence.

The decoder converts the power to DC, which drives the devices connected to the decoder, such as motors, LEDs, bulbs, and switch machines.

A microcontroller in the decoder analyzes the data in each packet to determine whether the packet is valid. Next, it checks to see if the address matches the decoder's address. If it matches, it analyzes the instruction and performs the task requested. Chapters 4 and 5 have more details on decoders.

Variations

Connections between cabs and the command station can be tethered (a cord), wireless, or part of an all-in-one system. Most manufacturers offer multiple throttle styles. Some are simple cabs designed to just operate trains;

DCC data flow

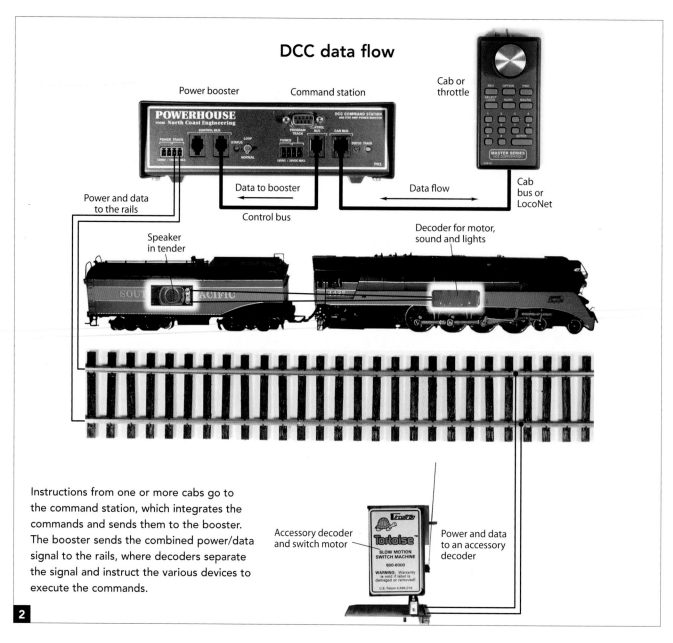

Cab or throttle

Power booster

Command station

Power and data to the rails

Data to booster

Control bus

Data flow

Cab bus or LocoNet

Speaker in tender

Decoder for motor, sound and lights

Instructions from one or more cabs go to the command station, which integrates the commands and sends them to the booster. The booster sends the combined power/data signal to the rails, where decoders separate the signal and instruct the various devices to execute the commands.

Accessory decoder and switch motor

Power and data to an accessory decoder

2

others allow programming and have more functions and a display panel.

Manufacturers use different protocols, to send information from cabs to the command station. Some protocols use polling; others use an interrupt scheme. With polling, the command station regularly polls each cab asking if it has any commands. With the interrupt scheme, the cab interrupts the command station to tell it that it has a command.

Lenz's interface uses a protocol called XpressNet, NCE's protocol is called Cab Bus, and the Digitrax protocol is LocoNet.

Likewise, not all manufacturers use the same method of transmitting

packets from the command station to the booster. Most systems use a separate connection between the two, but Digitrax integrates the booster signal into the same cable as used by the cabs.

Boosters range in power from less than 2 amps up to 10 amps, with 5 amps the most common size.

When a single booster powers a layout, a short circuit (such as a train running through a closed turnout) will shut down the entire layout until the short is cleared. By adding more boosters or circuit breakers, the shutdown can be limited to a single electrical block on the layout. (There's more information on boosters and circuit breakers in chapters 6 and 7.)

Bi-di communications

Bidirectional (bi-di) communication gives a decoder the ability to acknowledge a command or to talk back to the command station.

Bi-di communications are made possible with special decoders and block adapters. The block adapter briefly turns off power to the rails during the preamble of the packet, which signals the decoder to send a short special packet to the block adapter. The special packet from the decoder is then available through a connection on the block adapter. The decoder's capacitors supply decoder power during the short interval when the power is turned off.

CHAPTER THREE

Basic DCC technology

Information for DCC is sent over the rails in a similar fashion to the way data is transmitted over the Internet. On the Internet, data is grouped into packets. This chapter describes what's contained in DCC packets. The NMRA's DCC standards (Chapter 1) prescribe the format of data packets sent to the rails.

Denver & Rio Grande Western SD9 no. 5313 waits for GP35 no. 3050 to clear the crossing on the Bay State Model Railroad Museum layout. Digital Command Control allows operators to concentrate on operating trains instead of flipping switches for electrical blocks. *Lou Sassi*

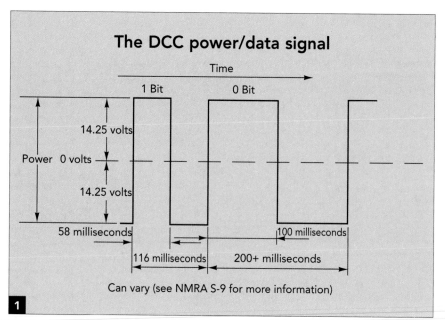

The DCC power/data signal

Time

1 Bit   0 Bit

14.25 volts

Power   0 volts

14.25 volts

58 milliseconds   100 milliseconds

116 milliseconds   200+ milliseconds

Can vary (see NMRA S-9 for more information)

1

The DCC signal is bipolar and switches between plus and minus. This keeps power continually on the rails, with data encoded by the length of time between the plus and minus transitions. The short signal is a "1" bit and the longer time is a "0" bit. The DCC standard is 14.25 volts.

Byte

Bit number	7	6	5	4	3	2	1	0
Bit value or weight	128	64	32	16	8	4	2	1

2

The "0" and "1" bits are assembled into groups of eight bits called a byte. Bits are numbered from right to left, and each has a value, or weight, which doubles for each increasing bit number. The sum of all bit values is 255.

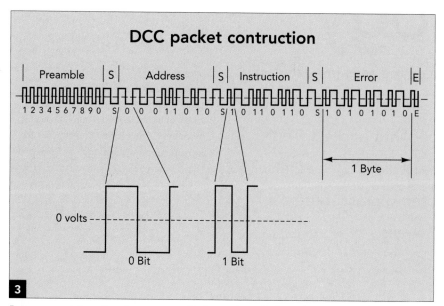

DCC packet contruction

| Preamble | S | Address | S | Instruction | S | Error | E |

1 2 3 4 5 6 7 8 9 0 S 0 0 0 1 1 0 1 0 S 1 0 1 1 0 1 1 0 S 1 0 1 0 1 0 1 0 E

1 Byte

0 volts

0 Bit   1 Bit

3

Bytes are put together in a group called a packet. Each packet starts with a preamble, followed by the address of the intended decoder. Next is the instruction. The packet ends with an error byte, which the decoder uses to verify the accuracy of the packet.

Power and data on the rails

The DCC system provides the power and necessary command signals to operate one or more locomotives, along with accessories such as turnouts and signals. The command instructions are imbedded in the electrical power that's fed to the rails to run locomotives or accessories. This is accomplished by rapidly changing the polarity from positive to negative. These positive-to-negative (plus-to-minus) transitions transmit the digital data, **1**.

The data is put into groups called packets. A decoder uses diodes to rectify the bipolar DCC signal. This recovers DC power independent of the data packet contents. A microprocessor in the decoder converts the power transitions to data.

The bit

Digital Command Control uses computer technology, so it shouldn't be surprising that the two share a similar nomenclature. The smallest element of digital information is a bit. Digital data is made up of 0s and 1s, each of which is one bit. This is because an electronic switch can be either on (1) or off (0). By combining bits into groups, we can make them indicate any number or value or have them represent any piece of information.

In DCC, time is used to define a 1 or 0—similar to the long and short whistle signals used by railroads, or the dot and dash of telegraphy. A bit is a cycle of one positive and one negative pulse. The 1 bit is shorter than the 0 bit—specifically, a "1" is between 55 and 61 microseconds long for a half cycle. The "0" is from 90 to 99,000 microseconds for a half cycle. The long 0, covered later in this chapter, is known as a stretched zero.

The byte

To make more sense out of 1s and 0s, they're put into groups of eight bits called bytes. Each of the eight bits in a byte has a position number and a weight or value. The first is bit no. 0 with a "weight" or value of 1. The count continues by doubling the weight of each bit to the last bit (no. 7) in the byte, which has a value of 128. The bits

These are examples of actual packets, which were captured using a program called DCCMON. This program monitors packets on the rails in real time.

Packet	Binary				Hex	Instruction
1	0 11111111	0 00000000	0 11111111	1	(FF 00 FF)	Idle
2	0 00100101	0 01111001	0 01011100	1	(25 79 5C)	Addr: 37 Forward speed 12/13
3	0 11010110	0 00001001	0 01111001	0 10100110 1	(D6 09 79 A6)	Addr: 5641 Forward speed 6/6
4	0 11001000	0 00111110	0 01010101	0 10100011 1	(C8 3E 55 A3)	Addr: 2110 Reverse speed 3/3
5	0 11011001	0 00110011	0 01110101	0 10011111 1	(D9 33 75 9F)	Addr: 6451 Forward speed 15/16
6	0 11000011	0 11110011	0 10000010	0 10110010 1	(C3 F3 82 B2)	Addr: 1011 Function Group 1
Byte	1	2	3	4		

The binary is the only part that is transmitted. The DCCMON program generated the hex and also added the description of the commands. The preamble isn't shown.

The binary commands also show the "0" bit separators between bytes and the "1" at the end of the packet. Packet 1 is an idle command that's used by the command station when there is no data to send. Packet 2 is a three-byte packet to locomotive no. 37 and is a speed command. Packets 3, 4, and 5 are four-byte packets to locomotives with long addresses. Direction and speed are included in these packets. Packet 6 tells locomotive no. 1011 to blow its horn.

are counted from right to left, **2**. The values of all 8 bits in a byte add up to 255. This will begin to make sense as you begin programming decoders using configuration variables (CVs), covered in chapter 5.

The packet

The Internet uses packets to transmit data. Packets include the recipient's address, followed by data. This is how each individual computer receives information on the Internet over a common line. Digital Command Control systems also use a form of packets to transmit data.

The command station assembles the DCC packets based on commands from a cab or throttle. Each packet has four parts: Preamble, address, instruction, and error code, **3**. All parts of the packet are separated by 0 bits, **4**.

The preamble is a minimum of ten 1 bits, and can be longer. More than eight bits are needed so the decoder can determine the start of a packet to get synchronized with the command

station. No other combination of ten or more 1 bits together is possible with the coding of the packets.

The address byte specifies the intended decoder. The address can be more than one byte long.

The instruction byte or bytes tell the decoder what task to execute, such as speed or function. This can also be more than one byte long.

The command station generates the error byte using the data in the packet. All of the bits in the packet are used to generate the error byte. The error byte is a unique number developed from the data in the packet.

Decoder operation

A decoder first gets into sync by finding a preamble. Once the decoder finds the preamble, it knows that the next parts are address, instruction, and error byte. All decoders receive the complete packet and then go through the same process the command station did to generate the error-code byte. If the error byte received from the command station matches the one

generated by the decoder, the packet is considered valid. If the error code doesn't match, the whole packet is rejected.

Once the decoder determines that the packet is valid, it checks the address. If the address matches the decoder's address, the decoder then checks the instruction byte. If the instruction—such as a change in speed—is valid for the decoder, it executes the instruction. If the instruction is invalid, nothing is done.

Types of packets

Packets are transmitted using a method known in the computer industry as "ship and pray"—the DCC packets are shipped out, and the system "prays" that they get to the destination. Rail/wheel contact makes for a poor electrical connection, so to ensure that the packet gets to the decoder, the command station sends multiple copies of the packet. The basic packet is only four bytes long, but with long addresses (four-digit instead of two-digit), the packet size is expanded.

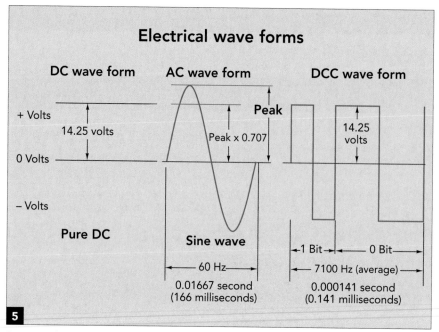

Electrical wave forms

DC wave form

+ Volts

14.25 volts

0 Volts

– Volts

Pure DC

AC wave form

Peak

Peak × 0.707

Sine wave

—— 60 Hz ——

0.01667 second
(166 milliseconds)

DCC wave form

14.25 volts

→1 Bit← →— 0 Bit —←

—— 7100 Hz (average) ——

0.000141 second
(0.141 milliseconds)

5

Because the DCC signal is a square wave, it's always either plus or minus, putting constant power on the rails. With DCC, the control tone is 100 percent of the power, so the DCC signal doesn't get lost.

The same is true with more complex instructions. The packet size can be from three to six bytes long, and a command station can transmit up to 150 packets per second. Normally, the response when you push a button is quicker than a blink of an eye. However, as packets get longer, it takes more time to transmit them. This typically isn't a problem with small layouts. On larger layouts with many operators and lots of packets to transmit, the command response time can slow noticeably.

New DCC specifications allow transmission of more information using fewer packets. For example, the old method of consisting (running two or more locomotives together using the same throttle) required the command station to send a command to each locomotive in a consist. Thus, a consist of four locomotives required four commands for each instruction. Advanced consisting now reduces this to a single packet, so the same command only uses one packet.

Another example will occur with bidirectional communication, which will allow decoders to tell the command station that a packet was received. (Bidirectional operation will need adapters and newer decoders designed for this function.)

Both of these changes will speed up operations by reducing the number of packets transmitted. Command stations also prioritize commands so new commands go out before older refresh commands. This means that some command stations can handle up to 120 operators.

Decoders and sound

Sound decoders are becoming increasingly common, both as stand-alone items and factory-installed in commercial models. This has been accomplished by the increasing amount of memory available for decoders. Most new sound decoders, featuring 16-bit sampling, have vastly improved sound quality compared to early decoders, which used 8-bit sampling.

DCC and DC

The combined DCC signal and power is at a much higher frequency than the 60 Hz of AC house current. And, because the DCC signal is a bipolar wave, it's always either plus or minus, which puts constant power on the rails, **5**.

The old Astrac system used AC on the rails and added a short high-frequency tone; the Dynatrol and

Onboard analog systems both added similar high-frequency tones to DC for control. These tones could get "lost" when there was a long run through a lot of wire. With DCC, the control tone is 100 percent of the power, so the signal can't get lost. However, the signal can be distorted in long cable runs.

Digital Command Control specifications make provisions for running decoder-equipped locomotives on standard DC power. A data bit in CV29 tells the decoder to either run or stop when straight DC is present. With the bit on, the decoder will run the locomotive when DC is on the rails, although it takes about 6 volts before the decoder has enough voltage to operate. This makes fine speed control difficult. If you drop below 6 volts, the decoder and locomotive stop.

You can also run a locomotive without a decoder on a few DCC systems, but it's not ideal. Command stations do this with a scheme that modifies the 0 bits, using what is known as the stretched zero (nearly 10 milliseconds). As long as the DCC signal is symmetrical, its average DC value on the rail is zero, so the motor in a locomotive without a decoder will not run in either direction. When the 0 bits are stretched either plus or minus, the average power becomes biased. The motor sees the bias as DC, and runs in the direction of the bias.

Only one locomotive on a layout can be controlled with the stretched zero. Extended use of DCC power on a locomotive without a decoder can overheat and damage a motor. Engines with coreless motors without decoders should never be placed on the rails with DCC power.

The stretched zero eats up a lot of time and slows down the number of packets the system can transmit. Not all manufacturers recommend this method of operation, and many systems don't implement this function. Digitrax and Lenz are among the few manufacturers that still use address 00 to run non-decoder-equipped locomotives.

CHAPTER FOUR

Basics of decoders

We're surrounded by microprocessors and microcontrollers in our daily lives. Microprocessors control our automobile engines and run our toothbrushes and wristwatches; even prototype locomotives use them. Name an electric device and it probably has a microprocessor buried in its circuits. Microprocessors are the brains of our decoders, cabs, and command stations, and their tiny size makes it possible to install decoders in Z scale locomotives.

Many newer locomotive models are equipped with plugs or removable circuit boards for easy decoder installation. On this Athearn HO model, the small jumper circuit board is removed (top) and a new decoder with a JST 9-pin connector added using a JST connector (at left on the decoder board). The decoder is an NCE D13SRJ. *Bill Zuback*

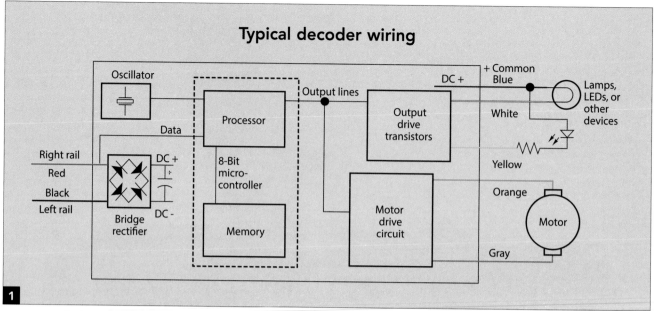

Typical decoder wiring

A decoder separates power from the data packets and then processes the data. The bridge rectifier converts the bi-polar DCC signal to DC to power the decoder. Information is extracted from the data signal by the microprocessor, which runs using a program stored in its memory. When commanded, the output lines turn on the lights, blow the horn or drive the motor.

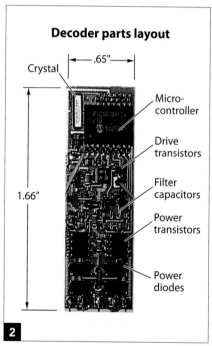

Decoder parts layout

Here's the layout of components for a typical DCC decoder. Decoder size has decreased and function increased significantly over the past few years and should continue to do so in the future.

Improved circuit technology has made sound a big part of the decoder market. The result has been wider variety of prototype-specific sounds and better sound quality. See Chapter 10 for more details on sound systems and decoders.

Microprocessors

Early DCC decoders were very basic, with limited addressing, lighting options, and motor control. Advancing technology allows more logic to be packed into microprocessors, **1** and **2**, which means many new features and functions at lower prices. Lighting possibilities have expanded, and many decoders incorporate sound capability. New wire interfaces and locomotives with plug-in sockets have simplified decoder installation. Locomotive manufacturers now offer models with decoders and sound systems preinstalled.

The microprocessor is a complex integrated circuit (IC) that can be programmed to do different tasks. Within the IC is the logic that makes it a computer: memory, input/output lines, and the ability to process instructions. A program stored in the microprocessor's memory retains the program even after power is off. This program, which is installed by the manufacturer, boots up the decoder and the program tells the microprocessor how to operate.

Transistors on the decoder board drive the output lines for the motor and functions. The transistors and diodes on the circuit board determine the power capacity of the decoder.

Part of the decoder's memory is used to store configuration variables (CVs) that can be modified by the user to customize the decoder's operation. Decoders come with factory-set default values in their CVs. This allows users to immediately use the decoder with few or no changes. Chapter 5 goes into details on CVs and programming.

Decoder types

Decoders come in two basic types: mobile and accessory (stationary). Mobile decoders, designed to be used in locomotives and other moving equipment, have outputs for a motor and lights. Sound decoders also have outputs for speakers or other accessories.

Mobile decoders come in many sizes, **3**, from extremely small decoders with low current ratings designed for N and Z scale locomotives to large decoders with high power ratings for O and G scales. Most decoders are designed to fit HO models. There are also small function-only decoders designed to control lights in cabooses and passenger cars.

Accessory decoders control trackside devices such as stall-motor or twin-coil switch machines. Since they're installed along the tracks or under the layout, accessory decoder size isn't important.

Most stationary decoders can operate more than one switch machine, and some can be programmed for use with different types of machines or to operate signals and lights.

Modern decoders feature increased function and decreased size. This results in decoders that are more complex and flexible. An example is the new drop-in QSI Titan sound decoder, which has 10 light connections on the board, plus two each for the motor and speaker, **4**. For more on light and sound see Chapters 9 and 10.

DCC plus DC operation

Some decoders allow locomotives to operate on either DCC or with a standard DC power pack. When used on standard DC systems, they require about 6 volts before the engine starts to move. This is because the decoder's electronics require that much voltage to function before it can operate. Bit 2 (value 4) in CV29 controls whether the decoder will respond to DC power. When off, the engine will not move on DC. To prevent a possible runaway, this bit should be turned off unless you're actually running the locomotive on standard DC.

Mobile decoder power ratings

Most decoders have three power ratings: the stall current of the motor, the rating of each function output, and the total power the decoder can handle. The last is the total of all current flowing through the decoder; the motor and all functions added together should not exceed this limit. For example, if you have a motor close to the motor current rating and add several 100-milliamp (0.1-amp) bulbs, you could easily exceed the maximum power rating of the decoder.

Check the rating of each decoder's function outputs. Even small N scale decoders have a rating of 100 milliamps, and some large scale decoders have a 1-amp rating on their function outputs. These outputs get their signal from the decoder's microprocessor and are driven by tiny transistors on the decoder circuit board. Light-emitting diodes (LEDs) are no

3

Decoders come in different formats and sizes. The Lenz decoder at top has components on both sides and uses the JST nine-pin connector. The NCE decoder at bottom is a drop-in replacement for the circuit board on many HO diesel models. Its connector tabs use slip-on plastic covers (included on the model's original board) to hold wires in place. This makes it easier to remove and install a new decoder.

problem for these outputs because their current requirement is constant and well below the rated output. Lamps are a much different story—see Chapter 9 for details on the differences between lamps and LEDs.

The semiconductors in decoders can generally tolerate a brief overload, but overloads at currents that greatly exceed their ratings will cause a failure. Higher voltage can also cause catastrophic failures. Most power boosters put out 13 to 14 volts, and the standard DCC voltage is 14.25. If you want to measure the DCC voltage on the rails, you'll need a meter that is true root-mean-squared (RMS) capable, such as the RRampMeter from Tony's Train Exchange. Standard voltmeters may give you inaccurate readings because the DCC wave form isn't a sine wave.

The output voltage of most decoders is 12 to 13 volts, with decoder circuits and resistance in layout wiring accounting for the voltage drop. If the booster voltage varies from 14 volts, the voltage from the decoder will also vary. The voltage can be lowered for N scale and increased for O and G scales. The voltage output from a decoder between the source (blue wire) and a function

output of the decoder is DC and can be accurately read by a standard DC meter.

DCC-ready locomotives

It's hard to find new locomotives that aren't either decoder equipped or set up for easy installation of a decoder. The term "DCC ready" is ambiguous, but used by many locomotive manufacturers. It generally means that the model has a socket for a plug-equipped decoder or a circuit board designed for a drop-in replacement of a circuit-board decoder. Either of these features makes it simpler to install a decoder. When buying a model, check its instruction manual to find which interface connector is used and determine what type of decoder will be needed. If you plan to install a sound decoder, you should also make sure there's room for a speaker.

A growing number of steam, diesel, and electric locomotives in N through G scales include factory-installed decoders as well as sound and lighting effects.

Decoder motor control

Decoders control the speed of a motor by rapidly turning the power on and off. Think of it this way: If a switch

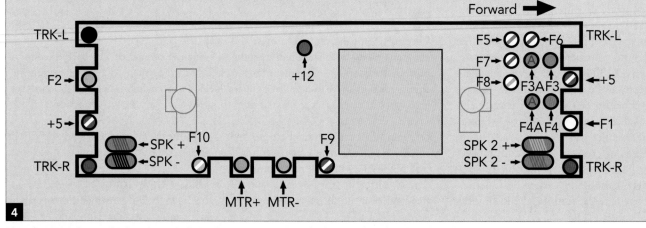

Simplified QSI Titan-A wiring diagram

Light Port/F#	Default behavior diesel	Default behavior steam
F1	Headlight	Headlight
F2	Reverse light	Reverse light
F3/F3A	Front Mars light	Front Mars light
F4/F4A	Rear Mars light	Front number board lights
F5	Front left ditch light	Front marker lights
F6	Front right ditch light	Rear marker lights
F7	Rear left ditch light	Front cab light
F8	Rear right ditch light	Rear cab light
F9	Front overhead beacon light	Firebox light 1
F10	Rear overhead beacon light	Firebox light 2

This diagram shows the layout and all the function connections that can be wired to the QSI Titan-A, a versatile modern sound decoder with 10 lighting outputs. The chart lists the functions for each connection.

connects a DC motor or lamp to a battery, and you turn the switch on and off very quickly, you can control the speed of the motor or the brightness of the lamp. This type of power control is called pulse width modulation (PWM), **5**. The rate of these pulses is controlled by CV9 (not found in all decoders). These pulses normally range from 50 to 250 Hz. In this frequency range, the motor can buzz or hum. By adjusting CV9, you can change the frequency to minimize the noise.

Because lower PWM frequencies can cause noise and hums in a locomotive, new decoders use a high-frequency motor drive. Manufacturers use different names for this type of drive circuit, but it's still PWM using frequencies from 15kHz to 40 kHz. In most cases, these frequencies are above the range of hearing. With this high frequency, the motor acts more like it's

running on DC. To get a smooth start with this type of power, many decoders use CV65 for a kick start, which helps torque compensation at low speeds. Some decoders use random-width pulses for smooth slow starts.

Back-electromotive-force control

Back-electromotive-force control (back-EMF) is a feature now found on most decoders. When a motor turns it acts as a generator, and the voltage generated by the motor turning is back-EMF.

Since the decoder turns the locomotive's motor on and off, the voltage generated by the motor can be read during the off part of the cycle. The decoder uses this reading to determine variations in motor speed. The decoder can increase the power if the motor slows, or decrease the power

if the speed increases, making this feature act like an automotive cruise control, **6**.

Back-EMF helps keep locomotives running smoothly at slow speeds, and can also smooth a binding steam engine mechanism. When used in a consist, however, a locomotive with back-EMF turned on can buck. This can be corrected by turning back-EMF off. Also, CV10 can be used to on some decoders to cut out the back-EMF function when the engine reaches a speed set by the value in this CV. Check the decoder's manual for more information on setting this CV.

Back-EMF does have some control over speed. I've found that when you go to the first speed step, the locomotive will just start to creep, even when CV2 hasn't been adjusted. Some decoders have a number of CVs that can be used to adjust the amount of back-EMF used by the decoder.

Do you need this feature? If you have a smooth-running locomotive and a reasonably flat layout, and you're satisfied with the locomotive's performance, back-EMF isn't going to do a lot for you. But if your layout has a lot of grades and you don't like constantly adjusting the speed, back-EMF can help. It can also help if you have a locomotive that doesn't run smooth at slow speeds. Just remember that back-EMF isn't a cure-all for poor-running locomotives.

Fighting dirty track

Poor wheel-to-rail contact is a problem in DCC just as it was in DC. Any dirt, grime, or oxidation on the rails can cause hesitation or stalling. When I was working on the first edition of this book, Lenz had just announced Uninterruptible Signal Processing, a module attached to its Gold Series decoder that would allow a decoder to keep processing commands when the power was interrupted, **7**. The success of Lenz's USP has led other manufacturers to produce similar super capacitor modules. Train Control Systems calls its module Keep-Alive, **8**, which is offered in different sizes and capacities. The firm recently announced that it has incorporated this technology in its new WOWSound decoders, **9**. NCE calls its super capacitor a No Halt Insurance Module.

So how do super capacitor modules work? When power is first applied, the capacitors need to be charged. To prevent overloading the DCC system, charging is slowed through a resistor. When the input voltage drops, power is supplied from the super capacitor to the decoder through a diode that bypasses the resistor.

I tested the Lenz USP in an Atlas HO diesel that had a Lenz Gold decoder. The first test was on Dave Parks' large Cumberland layout. I started by running the engine for a few minutes on the main line at speed step 1. This is a sure way to invite a stall, but the engine continued creeping along.

Seeking a better challenge, I asked Dave if he had any track that hadn't been cleaned. He pointed out a hard-

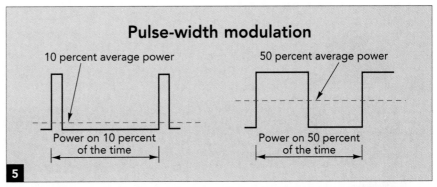

Pulse-width modulation

10 percent average power

Power on 10 percent of the time

50 percent average power

Power on 50 percent of the time

5

The decoder controls the locomotive motor by turning the power on and off at a high rate of speed. The frequency of this motor drive is set by CV9. Most new decoders use supersonic frequencies to minimize motor hum and vibration.

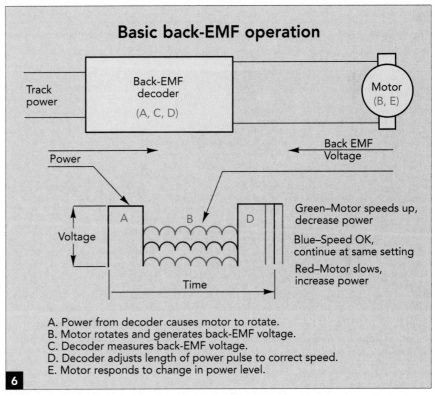

Basic back-EMF operation

Track power

Back-EMF decoder (A, C, D)

Motor (B, E)

Back EMF Voltage

Power

Voltage

A   B   D

Time

Green–Motor speeds up, decrease power

Blue–Speed OK, continue at same setting

Red–Motor slows, increase power

A. Power from decoder causes motor to rotate.
B. Motor rotates and generates back-EMF voltage.
C. Decoder measures back-EMF voltage.
D. Decoder adjusts length of power pulse to correct speed.
E. Motor responds to change in power level.

6

Back-electromotive-force control is great for slow starts and pulling heavy trains up a grade. The feature is normally turned on and off by a setting in a CV. This operates like cruise control in a car.

to-reach spur next to the engine facilities that hadn't been cleaned in years. We placed the engine on this track and it continued to creep along at speed step 1 without stalling!

I even tested the decoder with a 15" piece of tape on both rails. At medium speed, the engine ran across the tape without stopping. At speed step 1, the engine moved completely on the tape and continued about 1.5" before it finally stopped. Chapter 8 has additional information on super capacitors.

Accessory (stationary) decoders

A primary use of accessory decoders, **10**, is to operate switch machines. Some of these decoders can also be used to control lights and signals. Unlike mobile decoders that are designed to run one locomotive, some accessory decoders can operate multiple switch machines with separate addresses.

My layout has about every type of switch machine ever built. Choosing the right accessory decoder means

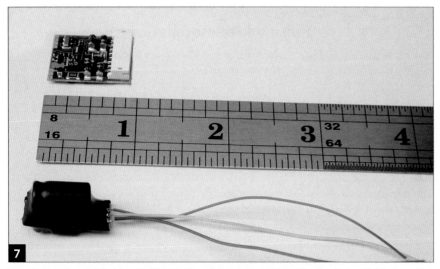

7

The Power-1 module is an add-on super capacitor module for the Lenz Gold decoder. It briefly provides power to the decoder when rail/wheel contact is broken.

8

Train Control Systems' KA2 module can be added to existing decoders. The super capacitor adds the Keep-Alive feature to a decoder, allowing it to keep processing commands when the power is interrupted. *Howard McKinney*

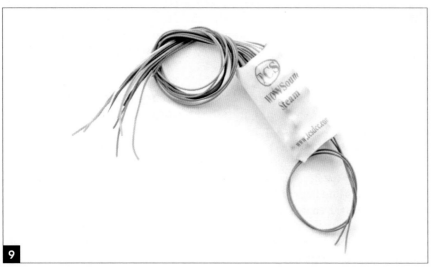

9

The new WOW 101 series of decoder from TCS uses 16-bit sound and incorporates an Audio Assist feature. Two models are available, one with the new super capacitor Keep-Alive function and one without it.

matching the decoder to the switch machine. An accessory decoder doesn't have to come from the same manufacturer is your DCC system. Chapter 8 has more information on doing this.

Accessory decoders use a different address range than mobile decoders. This means that an address of 37 for a mobile decoder is different from the address of 37 for an accessory decoder.

Key mapping

Decoders have multiple function outputs for lights and sounds, which can create conflicts between functions. For example, let's say you have two engines in a permanent consist using the same address. The lead locomotive has a decoder with multiple light outputs; the trailing locomotive has a sound decoder. As you approach a grade crossing, you want to turn on the ditch lights in the lead locomotive at the same time you sound the horn in the trailing unit. (Multiple decoders with the same address should be programmed separately.)

The horn function key works, but the ditch lights in the lead locomotive use a different function key. This is where key mapping can help. (Key mapping is an optional feature not found in all decoders.)

Key mapping is the ability to change the link from a function key input to an output in a decoder, **11**. Decoders come with default settings where each CV drives one output line (CV33 to CV46 are the standard CVs used for key mapping). You can set more than one output to turn on with a single function key by setting more bits "on" in the CV controlling the outputs.

Think of key mapping as a matrix with the function keys as the inputs and the decoder's output lines as the outputs of the matrix. Each point in the matrix is a bit in a CV that can be used to connect a key to the output line. Chapter 8 on lighting includes more information on key mapping.

Decoder models and manuals

Although your layout will use just one brand of DCC system, over the years you will likely accumulate

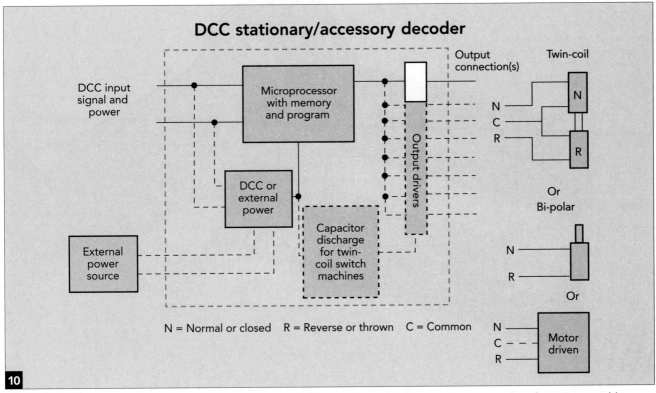

DCC stationary/accessory decoder

DCC input signal and power

Microprocessor with memory and program

DCC or external power

External power source

Capacitor discharge for twin-coil switch machines

Output drivers

Output connection(s)

Twin-coil

N

R

Or
Bi-polar

N

R

Or

Motor driven

N
C
R

N = Normal or closed   R = Reverse or thrown   C = Common

10

Stationary (accessory) decoders function like mobile decoders, but with a different address range and configuration variable numbers. The many styles of accessory decoders are designed to match the different types of switch machines. Some of these decoders will only drive one switch machine; others can drive up to eight. Stationary decoders can be powered from the rails or from a separate power supply.

decoders from several manufacturers. Each decoder has different features and may not take programming the same way as other decoders. Once you've programmed a decoder, save the instruction manual! At some point, you may need to reprogram the decoder, and the only source of information will be the manual. I keep mine in three-ring binders. Most manufacturers post manuals on their Websites, but they might not be available when you need them.

If you lose track of the brand and model of decoder installed in a locomotive, you can find the information by reading back two of the decoder's CVs: CV8 is a number assigned to each manufacturer by the NMRA, and CV7 is a version number for the decoder, assigned by the manufacturer. You can cross-reference these on the NMRA Website under RP-9.2.2, which lists manufacturers' CV8 numbers. The JMRI Decoder Pro freeware program uses these CVs to determine the manufacturer and software level of a decoder.

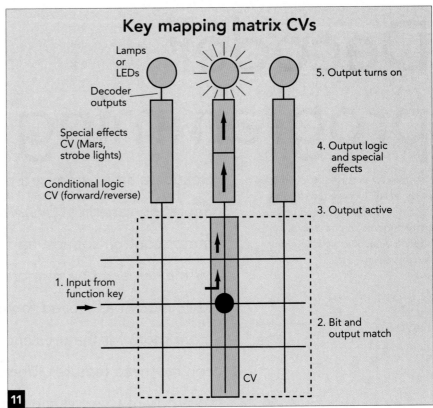

Key mapping matrix CVs

Lamps or LEDs

Decoder outputs

Special effects CV (Mars, strobe lights)

Conditional logic CV (forward/reverse)

1. Input from function key

CV

5. Output turns on

4. Output logic and special effects

3. Output active

2. Bit and output match

11

The standard location for key mapping is CV33 thru CV36 for functions F0 to F12. When a function key is pressed, the signal is fed to the matrix. When the input function line matches one of the CV bits, that output becomes active. If conditions are correct (such as forward direction), the output line is turned on.

CHAPTER FIVE

Decoder programming

An operator programs a locomotive using an NCE Power Cab throttle. Locomotive addresses and other characteristics can be changed by altering a decoder's configuration variables. *Jim Forbes*

Decoders are customized by programming their configuration variables (CVs). Addressing, special lighting, motor control, sounds, and consisting are all controlled by the value in one or more of a decoder's CVs. As technology has moved forward, newer decoders have more room for features and functions with more CVs to control these features. Understanding and knowing how to program CVs will allow you to get the most out of your decoders.

Decoders and programming

Decoders come with factory default values programmed into their CVs, so you can start operating without changing any CV values.

Each locomotive on a layout needs its own unique address, which is stored in its decoder's CVs. Mobile decoders come programmed to a default two-digit address of 3 (03). For many locomotives, all you need to do is change the address to avoid a potential conflict with other decoders, and you are ready to go.

All of the other functions of the decoder can be customized by changing the value in one or more CVs. Each CV's eight-bit bytes are stored in the decoder. Once a value is programmed into a CV, it will remain that way until changed again, even when power is turned off.

Decoders aren't the only programmable DCC device. Command stations also have programmable options, such as setting a fast clock's time and speed ratio. Routes and macros for controlling multiple accessory decoders are stored in the command station, along with other options, including factory reset. These options are all listed in the system manuals. Digitrax calls these options "switches."

A computer can make it easier to program a decoder, **1**. A free program called Java Model Railroad Interface (JMRI) is available over the Internet. The DecoderPro section of JMRI can be used for programming decoders and remembering the values in each CV, **2**.

CV numbering

Configuration variables are numbered from 1 to 512 for mobile decoders and 513 to 1024 for accessory decoders. Configuration variable numbers and their functions are assigned by the National Model Railroad Association (NMRA) as part of its DCC standards and recommended practices. Certain groups of CVs are reserved for manufacturer-specific functions. The effects of these CVs may vary among decoder models.

Each CV has eight bits numbered from 0 to 7, with 0 on the right, **3**. Each bit has a weight (value) of

Computer programs such as JMRI DecoderPro make it easy to program CVs. A portable programming track rests in front of the keyboard. *David Popp*

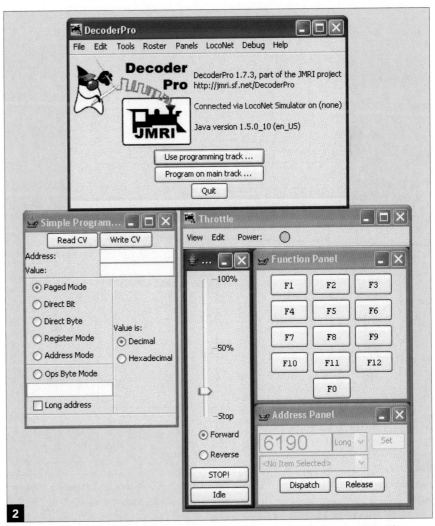

DecoderPro's on-screen graphics make it easy to visualize and program CVs. The program also reads all CVs so they can be filed in a roster for later use.

4	Decimal, hex, and binary	
Decimal	**Hex**	**Binary**
0	0	0000
1	1	0001
2	2	0010
3	3	0011
4	4	0100
5	5	0101
6	6	0110
7	7	0111
8	8	1000
9	9	1001
10	A	1010
11	B	1011
12	C	1100
13	D	1101
14	E	1110
15	F	1111

CV bit numbers are read from right to left. The weight (value) of each bit doubles for each position. Some decoders split the byte into two parts, called an upper and lower nibble.

0 when it is off, and each bit has a specific value when it's on. For example, when on, bit no. 0 has a value of 1, bit no. 1 has a value of 2, bit no. 2 has a value of 4, up to bit no. 7 with a value of 128. If only bit no. 7 is on, the CV total value is 128. If bit 0 (value 1) and bit 4 (value 16) are both on, the value in the CV is 17 (1+16).

When the value in a CV is changed, all eight bits are written back to the CV. This will become clearer as we go through this chapter.

The NMRA has four classifications of CVs: mandatory, meaning that all decoders must include this CV and use the assigned CV number; recommended, indicating CVs that should be in a decoder; optional, allowing a manufacturer to apply features not used by all decoders; and reserved, which are set aside for future use.

Three numbering systems

The trend in DCC is to use decimal (using numerals 0 to 9) numbering in newer documents and systems. But

This table only shows the values of the first four bits. Configuration variables have eight bits with a maximum value of 255 decimal (FF in hex, 11111111 in binary). In some DCC manuals, the values are shown as "102 (X66)." The first number is decimal, and the number in parentheses with the X is the value in hex. In this case the hex value is 66. I've also seen it listed as "66 HEX" or 0x66.

you should also be familiar with the two other numbering systems used in DCC: hex (hexadecimal) and binary.

Hexadecimal is a system based on 0 to 15, with the numbers 10 to 15 represented by the letters A through F. Binary, the common computer system, uses only 0 and 1. The table in **4** shows a comparison of the three systems. An example of hexadecimal use in decoders is in addressing. Two-digit decoder addresses run from 1 through 127. But isn't 127 three digits? In decimal, yes, but it's 7F in hex. The hex value of 7F is the reason numbers in this range are known as two-digit addresses. Four-digit addresses can range from 0000 through 9999. There's more on addressing later in this chapter.

Configuration variable samples

The chart on page 32 lists common CV assignments. Two-digit addressing uses CV1, and four-digit addressing

Methods of using CVs

Combination significant

Like a combination lock, the proper combination of bits turned on is needed to activate a function. Here bit 2 (weight 4), bit 3 (weight 8), and bit 6 (weight 64) are on, for a CV value of 76 (4 + 8 + 64).

Bit significant

Like a light switch, each bit turned on or off controls a separate feature in the CV.

Value significant

Like a volume control, the higher the value, the louder the volume.

5

Address CVs, like CV1 and CV17/18, are combination significant and need to have an exact value to define a locomotive's address. With bit-significant CVs (such as CV29), each bit needs to be set to turn a function on or off. Value-significant CVs control variables like sound volume levels. The exact value is not critical—a higher value means louder and lower means softer.

uses CVs 17 and 18. Two CVs are needed because a single CV is limited to a maximum value of 255. Thus, bits in CV18 are used to expand the value of CV17 to allow addressing up to 9999.

Configuration variable 19 is used for advanced consisting. Advance consists are limited to 127 addresses. Configuration variable 19 uses bits 0 to 6 for the address, with bit 7 used to tell the decoder the locomotive is running in the reverse direction from the other locomotives in a consist. With any value in CV19 other than zero the locomotive will not respond to motor commands but will respond to other functions. (A troubleshooting tip: If a locomotive is not responding to its normal address, try setting CV19 to 0.)

Types of CVs

To make CVs perform different tasks, they're used in three different ways. Configuration variables are either combination significant, bit significant, or value significant, **5**.

For example, CV1 uses a combination of bits that define the decoder's two-digit address. Only one combination of bits turned on will correctly define the address. This CV is combination significant.

In CV29, each bit turns a feature on or off. Setting a bit to 1 is like turning a switch on. This makes CV29 bit significant, **6**.

The CV that sets the volume of the horn in a sound decoder is value significant. To increase the volume, the value of the CV is increased. A change in value for this type of CV is just like changing the volume control on a radio.

Split CVs

Some decoders use split CVs, which allow one CV to control two functions. An example is the light control in some Digitrax decoders. Each CV controlling a function output uses the upper four bits (a group of four bits is called a nibble) to control how the CV works (such as forward/reverse or function on/off). The lower four bits control what the effect will be when on (such as flicker, strobe, or Mars light). SoundTraxx uses split CVs to control

CV29 Bit Functions		
Bit	Value	Description
0	1	Controls the normal direction of travel (NDOT); **on** to reverse the direction of travel.
1	2	**Off** for 14 speed steps, **on** for 28 Speed Steps (14-step speed to be dropped by NMRA)
2	4	**Off** will not run on DC power, **on** to run on DC power
3	8	**On** for advance acknowledgment
4	16	**Off** for standard speed table, **on** for alternate table (CV 67-94)
5	32	**Off** for two-digit addressing, on for four-digit addressing.
6	64	Reserved for future use by the NMRA
7	128	**Off** for multi-function decoder, **on** for accessory decoder

Sample Value 10101110							
Bit (Value)	7 (128)	6 (64)	5 (32)	4 (16)	3 (8)	2 (4)	1 (2)	0 (1)
Example	1 (on)	0 (off)	1 (on)	0 (off)	1 (on)	1 (on)	1 (on)	0 (off)

In this example, the binary value of 10101110 ("174" in decimal or "AE" in hexadecimal) tells us that an accessory decoder is being used (bit 7 on) with four-digit addressing (bit 5 on).

6

CVs are numbered from 1 to 1024. This chart shows functions for CV29. A complete listing of CVs can be found in NMRA RP 9.2.2. Many CVs are "manufacturer unique" so they can be used for special features such as sound and lighting. Check each decoder's manual for detailed information on the CVs for that decoder.

two different sound levels. When you change one of these split CVs, you must write back all eight bits to the CV. You may have to determine the value needed using hex, then program the value using decimal.

Indexed CVs (QSI)

The number of features and sounds available in mobile decoders have increased substantially in the last few years. This is great, but the problem is that the number of features exceeds the number of function keys available to run them and the number of CVs available to program features. With 28 functions available, this should help this function limitation.

Manufacturers deal with this limitation problem in different ways. Function keys can be set up to do different things depending on whether an engine is moving forward, backward, or is in neutral (stopped).

Volume levels need to be set for each of the added sounds. QSI solved this by making a matrix using only two CVs. The resulting 256 x 256 matrix

provides 65,536 unique solutions, which should be large enough to handle future expansion.

To program one of these indexed CVs you need to set a primary and secondary index, and then set a value. For a complete explanation read the QSI DCC manual (downloadable from the QSI Website).

This type of indexing is now in NMRA S-9.2.2. The indexing uses CV31 as the primary and CV32 as secondary CV.

Decoder program modes

Programming a decoder is a matter of changing the value of its CVs. The two basic methods of programming are service mode and operations mode.

Service mode programming requires use of a programming track. This is a section of track with its own connection to the command station. It must be electrically isolated from the rest of the layout. The programming track allows you to change the value of a CV and also lets you read back the CV value from the decoder. For

Consisting

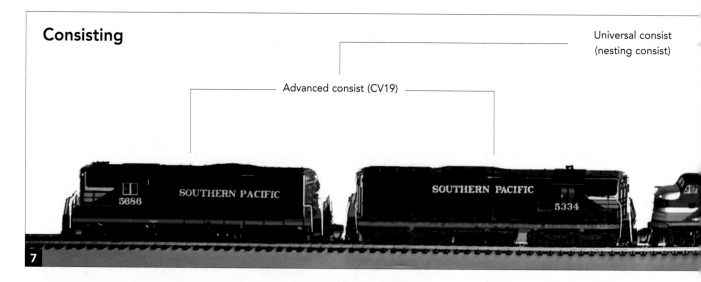

Universal consist (nesting consist)

Advanced consist (CV19)

7

example, if you have forgotten a decoder's address, you can read it back on the programming track.

The programming track is the best place to set up a new decoder, and also to check new installations for short circuits. The programming track output provides a limited amount of power—enough to run the decoder and program CVs, but not run the motor or illuminate lamps. The limited power protects the decoder from damage in case of a short circuit.

The service mode feature isn't included in all command stations or decoders. The NMRA defines a unique set of packets for use in the service mode.

The method of extracting (reading back) the CV value from a decoder on the programming track is very ingenious. The command station "asks" the decoder what the value is in

a CV. It starts by asking the decoder if the value in a CV is 1. If the value in the CV doesn't match, the decoder does nothing. The command station continues to change the asked value until there's a match between the asked value and the value in the CV. When the asked value matches the decoder's CV value, the decoder responds by briefly turning on the motor. (Sound-only decoders use the speaker.) This causes a sudden increase in current, which the command station senses. The higher the value in the CV, the longer it takes to determine the CV value. When the value in the decoder and command station match, the locomotive will lurch or there will be a short kick in the motor.

The programming track uses a broadcast address, so any decoder on the track will be programmed. That's why it's important to make sure that

only the engine you want to program is on the programming track.

The capability of newer sound decoders has increased the amount of current needed on the programming track. This can result in a "Can't Read CV" message. Super capacitor modules can also interfere with the read-back function. It's a good idea to program a decoder before connecting the super capacitor.

Ops mode programming

Operations mode (sometimes called "ops" or "on-the-fly") programming allows you to change a CV while the locomotive is on the main line. For example, if the whistle volume is too low, you can change it while listening to it. Acceleration or deceleration rates can also be changed. This is handy when you need a quicker response rate in a yard or a longer rate on the main

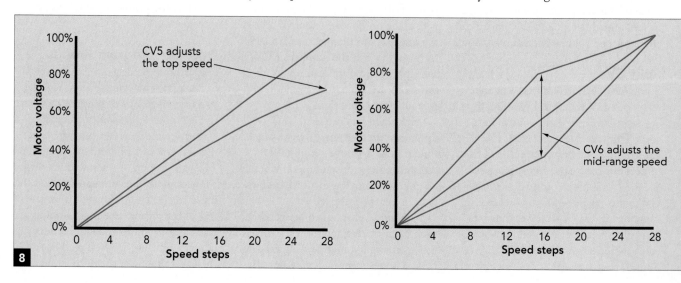

8

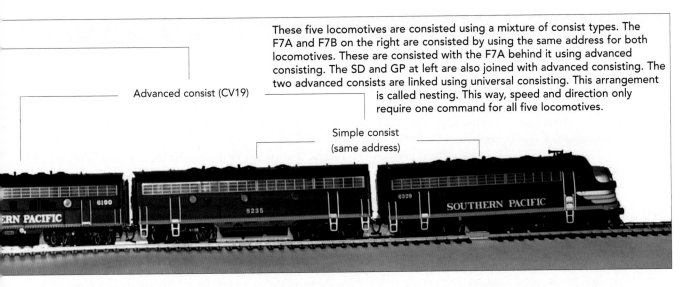

These five locomotives are consisted using a mixture of consist types. The F7A and F7B on the right are consisted by using the same address for both locomotives. These are consisted with the F7A behind it using advanced consisting. The SD and GP at left are also joined with advanced consisting. The two advanced consists are linked using universal consisting. This arrangement is called nesting. This way, speed and direction only require one command for all five locomotives.

Advanced consist (CV19)

Simple consist (same address)

line. Operations mode programming is a write-only operation and doesn't currently have read-back capability. Some sound decoders give a verbal response in ops mode.

Programming methods

DCC systems "talk" to the decoder during programming through a number of different techniques. Address-only programming was used to program CV1 only. Register-mode programming handles a group of CVs. Neither of these older methods are used much today. Paged CV addressing is the preferred technique, and is used by most manufacturers.

These programming methods are generally transparent to the user—most DCC systems will automatically test a decoder to determine which method will work, and will use the appropriate one.

Forward/backward

The bits in CV29 are like a group of switches, **5**. Setting a bit to 1 is like turning a switch on. Bit 0 (value 1) is the NDOT (normal direction of travel), and is used so the direction set by the cab (throttle) matches that of the locomotive.

When bit 0 is off, the locomotive will travel forward with a forward command. If you have a model with the motor wired backward, or a diesel locomotive designed to run long-hood forward, a forward command will cause the locomotive to run in reverse. Turning bit 0 on will cause the locomotive to operate in the reverse direction. Configuration variable 29 also controls two- and four-digit addressing, alternate speed table selection, and several other decoder features.

Addressing a decoder

Addressing is one of the most important capabilities of DCC. By assigning each locomotive a unique address, you can then send a command to any individual decoder mobile or accessory on a layout.

Addressing is very flexible. A decoder will respond to up to four different addresses: either the original two-digit address (from 1 to 127) stored in CV1 or the four-digit address (1 to 9999) stored in CVs 17 and 18; the broadcast address of 0, used for emergency stop when you need to halt all engines on a layout (and also used on the programming track); and advance consisting using CV19.

New decoders come with a default two-digit address of 3 (03). Four-digit addressing lets the locomotive's number be the decoder's address. This makes addresses easy to remember.

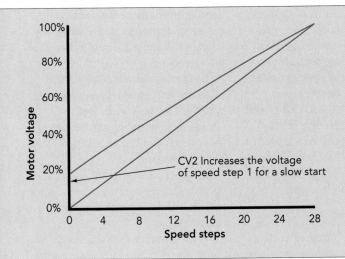

CV2 Increases the voltage of speed step 1 for a slow start

Speed control

CVs 2, 5, and 6 allow you to adjust the speed of a locomotive over the range of speed steps. CV2 adjusts the starting voltage, which can be set so the engine starts to roll with speed step 1. Configuration variable 5 sets the top speed at speed step 28, and CV6 adjusts the speed gradient by setting mid-range speeds. Most decoders have CV2; CVs 5 and 6 aren't as common.

One of the most important CVs in a decoder is CV29. This CV sets up a lot of the basic decoder functions (see chart **5**). Each bit in the 8-bit CV controls some basic operations of the decoder. Once you decide how you want the decoder to function, you must determine which bits should be set. Some DCC systems walk you through setting up CV29. Others require setting the whole CV. In this case you need to determine the total value for CV29 by adding up the value of the bits.

Each of the 8 bits in CV29 has a separate function. The 8 bits are numbered 0 to 7. Here is a list of the function of each bit in CV29 (bit weight in parentheses).

Bit 0: (1) Basic direction of the locomotive. Used to reverse the normal direction. One use is to run a diesel long end first. Normally off (0).

Bit 1: (2) Decoders originally had just 14 speed steps. Today's decoders use 28 or 128 speed steps but retain the 14 speed steps for compatibility. On contemporary decoders, this bit should be set on (1).

Bit 2: (4) This bit allows a locomotive to operate on either DCC or DC. Unless you have a very good reason to use the locomotive on both DCC and DC, leave this bit off (0).

Bit 3: (8) Used with DCC systems that have a feedback feature. Leave bit off (0).

Bit 4: (16) Most decoders have an adjustable speed table using CV67 to CV94. This bit switches from the standard speed settings to the decoder's built-in adjustable table. This bit is only on (1) when using the alternate speed table.

Bit 5: (32) Standard addressing uses CV1 as a two-digit address. (1 to 128). 128 is three digits, but in hex (7F) it's only two digits. With this bit on, CV17 and CV18 are used for four-digit addressing.

Bit 6: (64) This bit is reserved by the National Model Railroad Association for future use. Leave off (0).

Bit 7: (128) This bit defines the decoder as a locomotive multifunction mobile (0) or accessory decoder (1). Leave off for locomotives.

When you set an engine for four-digit addressing (CV17/18) from two-digit addressing (CV1), CV29 bit 5 must be turned on. Most DCC systems do this automatically, but if you make the address change and it doesn't work, CV29 is the first place to look. Another cause for engines not to respond is if CV19 is set for consisting and has a value other than zero.

Address ranges

Not all DCC systems use the full range of addressing. Most have a two-digit range of 1 to 127. If you program an address in the four-digit range of 0001 to 0127 in one system, it may not work on systems with limited-range four-digit addressing. Some systems limit the two-digit address to 1 to 99. In some systems, 120 is a two-digit address, while 0120 is handled as a four-digit address. The table on page 34 (Chapter 6) shows the range of addresses for several DCC systems.

Remember that address 120 is called a two-digit address because the range in hex is 00 to 7F. The 7F hex is equal to 127 decimal.

Four-digit addressing

The maximum value of a CV is 255, so to have addresses up to 9999, decoders use a pair of CVs (17 and 18). Most DCC systems will automatically compute the correct values for these two CVs. The top two bits (6 and 7) in CV17 always have a value of 1, which adds 192 to the value of CV17. Most DCC systems put the correct values in CV17 and CV18 based on the locomotive address. Configuration variable 29 bit 5 (weight 32) must to be turned on for four-digit addresses.

Assigning address in clubs

In model railroad clubs where members bring their own locomotives, identifying two locomotives that are identical but have separate owners can be a problem. The narrow gauge group that I was in solved this problem by using the decoder address. Each member was assigned a number from 0 to 9. If you had a locomotive with an address of 384 and your assigned number was 5, the decoder address would be 5384. This only works for groups with 10 or fewer members.

Another way is to use CVs 105 and 106 to identify a locomotive. These two CVs are for a user identification numbers like your NMRA membership number. These two are optional CVs and may not be in all decoders.

Consisting

Consisting means running more than one locomotive with a single command.

An example would be if you have three diesels pulling a single train. DCC provides several ways to build consists.

With today's decoders, most modelers use four-digit addressing for their locomotive and reserve the two-digit address for use in consisting with CV19.

Basic consisting is the simplest way: This is simply programming more than one decoder to the same address. For example, if you have an F7A and F7B that always operate together, giving the same address to both ensures that they will follow the same commands, **7**.

This is also the way to control two decoders in the same locomotive. For example, if you use a high-current motor decoder and a separate sound decoder in the same locomotive, programming them to the same address will cause them to function as one decoder.

Basic consisting is done on the programming track by programming each decoder separately. Basic consisting is portable, meaning the locomotives can be moved to another DCC layout and controlled the same way. Any command to this type of consist, such as headlight, horn, or whistle, will be executed by all engines in the consist.

With universal (sometimes called "brute force") consisting, locomotives

Decoder reset commands

Manufacturer	Manufacturer ID in CV8	CV for Reset + Value	
Lenz	99	CV8 = 33	
NCE	11	CV30 = 2	
Digitrax	129	CV8 = 8	
LokSound (ESU)	151	CV8 = 8	
TCS	153	CV8 = 8	
TCS	153	CV30 = 2	
SoundTraxx DSDLC, DSX	141	CV8 = 8	CV30 = 2
SoundTraxx Tsunami	141	CV8 = 8	CV30 = 2
MRC*	143	CV125 = 1	
QSI*	113	See Text	

*A programming track current booster, such as the Tony's Train Exchange PowerPax or the SoundTraxx PTB-100 will help in reading back CVs. If your decoder doesn't work, try resetting it. A high percentage of decoders returned to the factory as defective only need to be reset.

with separate addresses are combined into one consist. Once the consist is set up by the command station, it sends out a separate command to each locomotive in the consist. Thus, changing the speed in a consist of four locomotives requires the command station to send four separate commands. The operator sets universal consisting using a cab, and the method works with both older and newer decoders. This type of consist can be used only on the DCC system that set it up—if you move the locomotives to another layout, you will need to consist them again.

Advanced consisting is the newest method and is generally the best choice for setting up consists. It uses CV19 in each decoder in a consist to control all of the locomotives in that consist. Advanced consisting uses two-digit addresses from 1 to 127. Bit 7 in CV19 is used to indicate the locomotive's direction in the consist.

Advanced consisting (CV19) is set up using a cab. The advantage is that the command station only needs to send out one command to the consist for all locomotives to respond. This cuts down on the number of data packets needed to control a consist. When the consist is broken up, CV19 is reset to 0. (If you ever have an engine that doesn't respond to its address, try setting CV19 to 0.)

With advanced consisting, you can send commands (such as headlight or horn) to the lead locomotive using its four-digit address, and the command

will be ignored by other engines in the consist.

Four additional CVs work with advanced consisting: CVs 21 and 22 control which decoder functions will operate when a locomotive is in a consist, CV23 controls the consist acceleration rate, and CV24 controls the consist braking rate.

Advanced consists are portable and can be moved from layout to layout. A potential problem with advanced consisting is that the two-digit consist address looks the same as a two-digit locomotive address. Be sure the consist address used isn't the same as a locomotive with the same two-digit address. If possible, use two-digit addresses for consists and four-digit addresses for locomotives. This avoids conflicts. Some systems allow four-digit addressing from 0001 to 9999. This lets you use two-digit addressing for consists without conflicts.

A nesting consist is a combination of consisting methods to run a single consist. For example, you might have two advanced consists that you'd like to run as a single consist. To do this, just make a universal consist using the two advanced-consist addresses.

Speed control

Speed control, a flexible DCC feature, can be used to make a locomotive's speed more realistic. Digital Command Control started with 14 speed steps, but this was later increased to 28 speed steps, making the 14-speed-step obsolete. The 28 steps (with a 128

speed-step option) is now standard. Digital Command Control decoders come with a standard linear speed table.

There are three CVs to adjust the speed of a locomotive, **8**. Use CV2 to set the starting voltage. This comes in handy when you have an engine that needs a little extra boost to get started. (Back-EMF also helps with starting.) Two other optional CVs, found on most decoders, come in handy: CV5 is used to set the top speed, with CV6 used for mid-range speeds. All are handy for making quick speed adjustments. Check each decoder's manual for the availability of CVs 5 and 6.

You can also adjust the speeds of locomotives so that all locomotives in a consist operate at the same speed when set to the same speed step. Configuration variables 67 to 94 make up the alternate speed table, which can be used to adjust the 28 steps to provide more precise speed control. Speed control using these 28 CVs can also provide 128 speed steps. I've seen as many as 2048 speed steps available in a decoder, even though these aren't yet supported by all DCC systems. Decoders compute the 128 speed-step values by averaging the difference in the values between the 28 steps. Check your decoder manual to see if CVs 67 through 94 are supported.

The alternate speed table is turned on with CV29 bit 4. Java Model Railroad Interface's DecoderPro program allows you to customize the

There are two basic methods of programming a decoder: Using the programming track or using program-on-the-main (POM) or on-the-fly programming.

Here's a step-by-step description of programming a decoder on the programming track using an NCE Power Cab (other systems will vary—check your manual for specifics).

Place the engine on the programming track. With power on, press the PROG/ESC key four times until you see:
SEL MODE XX:XXAM
USE PROGRAM TRK
Press ENTER. You should then see:
PROG TRK
1=STD 2=CV 3=REG

Press 2 for CV programming and the display will be:
PROG CV
PROG CV NUM:
Enter the CV number to be programmed—for example, 1
for the short address:
PROG CV
-----WAIT-----
The response after the wait will be either the value in CV1 or:
PROG CV
CANNOT READ CV
Sometimes sound decoders have difficulty reading back the value on the program track. If it read OK, the display will show:
PROG CV
CV VALUE = XX
Press ENTER and then
PROG CV

CV NUM 001 = XX
Press ENTER, and the number will be programmed into CV1. The display will come back asking for the next CV to be programed:
PROG CV
PROG CV NUM:
When you're finished, press ESC/PROG to get out of the programming mode.
Program-on-the-main, or on-the-fly programming, lets you program CV settings while the engine is in use on the layout (not on the programming track). With this method, it's not possible to read back CV values. Also, unlike program-track programming, you must use the address of the locomotive to be programmed.

Here's an example, again using the NCE Power Cab. Press ESC/PROG once and the screen shows:
SEL MODE XX:XXXM
PROGRAM ON THE MAIN
Press ENTER and you'll see:
OPS PROG XX:XXXM
PROG LOCO: 1234
Be sure that the proper locomotive number is selected, or you may program the wrong one. Press ENTER and the display is:
LOC:1234 XX:XXXM
1=ADR 2=CV 3=CFG
There are other options if you press ENTER, or if you know the option number, just press the number key. There are nine options. Option 9 allows you to set individual bits in a CV. The screen looks like this for option 9:
CV: 00X 76543210
BITS 00000000
Type the number of the bit to change, and it will change to a 1; type the same number (1, 0) again to toggle it back to a 0. Press ENTER to program the CV and more CVs, or ESC/PROG to return to standard operation. For the 2=CV mode simply press 2, then the CV number, and then the value. ENTER to program and return to normal operations.

values in these CVs on-screen using a mouse, then send the settings to the decoder.

Another way to control speed is with CV25 (an optional CV used in some decoders). This CV sets a speed-curve profile. Programming a value in this CV turns on one of the predefined speed profiles in the decoder.

You can also adjust the speed of a

locomotive when it's in a consist using CV23 for acceleration and CV24 for deceleration.

Some decoders now have a switching speed option activated with a function key. When activated, the speed is reduced by half, and the acceleration and deceleration are also reduced. This is handy when using a road locomotive as a switcher.

Simplified decoder programming

It's sometimes difficult to determine which CV controls what feature. If you get lost in the translation from CV to function, help is available. The DecoderPro program helps by putting the function name on the screen and then letting you enter a value or move a slider with a mouse to change

Accessory Decoders				
CV No.	CV function	Requirements	Default Value	Description
513	Low order address bits	Mandatory	–	High bits in CV521
519	Manufacturer version number	Mandatory	–	Version of the decoder
520	Manufacturer ID value	Mandatory	–	Assigned by NMRA
521	High order address bits	Mandatory	–	Low bits in CV 513
541	Configuration data	Optional	–	Like CV29 for accessory decoders

a CV value. DecoderPro is updated frequently and is free over the Internet (jmri.sourceforge.net). As new decodes become available, a new profile is set up online.

Accessory decoder programming

Accessory decoders use a different address range than mobile decoders: from 1 to 2044 (but not all DCC systems use the full range), **9**.

Programming an accessory decoder is different than programming a mobile decoder. Instead of using a programming track, the decoder is set to program mode with a programming jumper, wire, or push button. When in program mode, the decoder waits until the command station sends an accessory packet, then it stores the address in the decoder. The temporary jumper is removed, and the decoder retains the address information.

There are many variations on programming accessory decoders, so always check the decoder's manual for the correct procedure.

Accessory decoder commands

Some of the accessory decoders used for switch machines also have the ability to operate more than one switch machine with a single command. Some systems also have the ability to set up routes through a number of switch machines. NCE calls them "macros" and Digitrax refers to them as "routes." In either case, this allows you to assign a number to a route that will operate multiple switch machines (see your system manual for more information on these functions.)

In my main yard there is one track entering and one track exiting the area,

9

Accessory decoders can control switch machines, as shown above, or many other accessories on a layout.

so a number of routes need to be set up. I placed a map of the yard on the layout's fascia that shows the different switch and route numbers. The numbers are color coded so operates can differentiate between switches and routes.

I have a crossover between East and West main lines that's controlled by two solenoid switch machines. These machines need to operate together as either reverse for the crossover or normal for the mainline. I installed separate decoders for each machine and programmed them to the same address. A single command operates both switch machines.

NCE makes a Mini Panel that allows you to program operations on switch machines. This type of panel can be programed for many flexible routes. You can even set up an N-X (eNtrance-eXit) control panel. This is a type of panel used on prototype railroads for complex switching arrangements. The operator presses one button for the entrance to the yard and a second button for the exit route.

When a valid route is detected, the panel issues the proper commands to align the appropriate turnouts for the route. There are some provisions for setting this up in JMRI with PanelPro.

Nonfunctional decoders

Many decoder manufacturers report that a good share of decoders sent in for repair only need to be reset to factory default to be restored. If you have a decoder that's not functioning, there's a way to rescue it without sending it back to the manufacturer.

The read-only CV8 is mandatory and contains the manufacturer's identification number (see page 29). Writing to this CV will not erase the identification number. Instead, it can cause the decoder to be reset to factory settings. The reset response varies between manufacturers. Some flash the lights as a response.

If you have a QSI decoder, refer to the decoder manual for information on resetting. By using different CVs, it's possible to reset only part of the decoder while retaining other parts.

Common configuration variables (CVs) in decoders

CV No.	CV function	Requirements	Default Value	Description
1	Primary (two-digit) address	Mandatory	3	Address range 01 to 127
2	Start voltage	Recommended	0	Sets minimum starting voltage
3	Acceleration rate	Recommended	0	Speed-up rate
4	Deceleration rate	Recommended	0	Slow-down rate
5	Voltage high (max speed voltage)	Optional	1	Sets maximum speed
6	Voltage mid (mid-speed voltage)	Optional	1	Sets mid-range speed
7	Manufacturer version number	Mandatory	–	Version (model) of the decoder
8	Manufacturer ID value (read only)	Mandatory	–	Number assigned by the NMRA
9	Pulse-width modulation time	Optional	0	Controls PWM time
10	EMF feedback cutout	Optional	–	Speed step to turn off back-EMF
11	Packet time out	Recommended	–	Max time to continue speed with no packets
13	Alternate mode function status F1-F8	Optional	–	Function status in alternate power mode
14	Alternate mode function status F9-F12	Optional	–	Function statue in alternate power mode
15	Lock feature	Optional	–	Value must match CV16 to unlock
16	Lock feature	Optional	–	Value to match CV15
17/18	Extended (four-digit) address	Optional	–	CV29, bit 5 "on" to use. †
19	Consist (two-digit) address	Optional	–	Range 01 to 127; 0 = not in consist.
21	Consist address active for F1-F8	Optional	–	Defines function use in consist
22	Consist address active for FL and F9-12	Optional	–	Defines lights and function use in consist
23	Consist acceleration adjustment	Optional	--	Adjustment when in consist
24	Consist deceleration adjustment	Optional	–	Adjustment when in consist
25	Speed rate profile	Optional	–	Selects a speed rate profile (rarely used)
29	Configuration data no. 1	Mandatory	–	Sets many decoder features ††
30	Error information	Optional	–	Decoder error information
31	Index primary number	Optional	–	Primary number for indexed CVs
32	Index secondary number	Optional	–	Secondary number for indexed CVs
33-46	Key mapping F0-F12	Optional	–	Sets function key input to output device
49-64	Manufacturer unique	Optional	–	–
65	Kick start	Optional	–	Assists in starting
66	Forward trim	Optional	128	Extra power when in forward
67-94	Alternate speed table	Optional	–	CV29, bit 4 "on" to use this table
95	Reverse trim	Optional	128	Extra power when in reverse
105	User ID No. 1	Optional	–	Can be your ID number
106	User ID No. 2	Optional	–	Second ID number

† In some systems, the four-digit address range is 0001 to 9999; in others it is 128 to 9983 or 000-9999. Check your system manual.

†† CV29 bit functions (all decoders don't have all of these features); see chart on page 24.

CHAPTER SIX

How to choose a DCC system

You'll make the best decision when selecting a Digital
Command Control system if you first consider how the
system will be used. Think about the size and scale of
your layout, the number of operators who will be running trains, and the features that are important to you.
In this chapter we will explore the various factors for
researching the purchase a DCC system.

Systems from various manufacturers
have differing features and displays.
The entry level Digitrax Zephyr (center)
includes a cab on the control station;
others, such as the MRC Prodigy
Advance2 and NCE Power Pro, rely on
handheld cabs. (The new Zephyr Xtra has
more push buttons.) *Jim Forbes*

	NCE DCC Twin	Digitrax Zephyr Xtra	NCE Power Cab	MRC Prodigy Express	Lenz Set 90	Lenz Set 100	Digitrax Super Chief Xtra	NCE PowerPro	CVP EasyDCC
Number of cabs	2 + 2	Up to 20	Up to 3	Up to 32	Up to 31	Up to 31	Up to 120	Up to 63	Up to 31
Type of speed control	Knob (2)	Knob	Key/knob	Knob	Knob	Key	2 knobs	Knob/key	2 knobs
Wireless cab options	Yes with added cabs	Yes with added cabs	Yes with added cabs	Yes with added cabs	Yes with XPA adapter	Yes with XPA adapter	Yes	Yes	Yes
Maximum number of addresses	2 on the unit, more with added cabs	9000+ (4-digit) 127 (2-digit)	9999 (4-digit) 127 (2-digit)	9999 (4-digit) 127 (2-digit)	9999 (4-digit) 99 (2-digit)	9999 (4-digit) 99 (2-digit)	9000+ (4-digit) 127 (2-digit)	9999 (4-digit) 127 (2-digit)	9999 (4-digit) 99 (2-digit)
Total function keys	9	28	28	28	16	12	28	28	13
Program track read/write	No	Yes	Yes	Yes	Yes	Yes	Yes	Yes	Yes
Output current in amps	3	3	2	1.6	5	5	5	5	7
Operates accessory decoders	No	Yes	Yes	No	Yes	Yes	Yes	Yes	Yes
Transformer included	Yes	Yes	Yes	Yes	No	No	No	No	No
Length of warranty	One year	One year	One year	One year	Up to 10 years	Up to 10 years	One year	One year	90 days
Power booster available	No	Yes	Yes	Yes	Yes	Yes	Yes	Yes	Yes
Basic List Price	$160	$225	$199	$170	$442	$497	$455	$530	$275

This comparison primarily features DCC starter systems. The simpler, more-basic systems are on the left; more advanced systems are on the right.

Selecting a system

There are two basic types of controls for DCC systems. The first group is starter systems that include a stationary throttle. The second group includes systems with tethered or wireless walkaround throttles.

Stationary throttles work for small layouts where it's easy to reach everything from one position. If you only have to walk a short distance, a tethered throttle is a viable option. If you have to walk longer distance to reach other parts of a layout, a wireless throttle is the best option. Most stationary all-in-one systems can be expanded with tethered or wireless throttles. This is a good way to get started into DCC and expand later on without wasting your money.

There are two items to check when purchasing a DCC system outside of the United States. Is the power supply compatible with your country's voltage and frequency? Some of the new power supplies are universal and will work on most almost all voltages and cycles (50/60 Hz). Also, check if the plug on the power cord is compatible.

It's also important to check if the radio frequency used in the wireless throttle is licensed for use in your country. If the wireless cab isn't licensed, a Wi-Fi cab using smartphones and tablets may work. See Chapter 12 for more information.

Selecting a brand

When buying a computer, it can be helpful to buy the same kind as your friend or neighbor. That way you have someone to talk to if problems occur on your computer.

The same thing applies to buying a DCC system. If you're in a club or have friends who use one brand, consider that brand. Also, check out information online. Several Yahoo! user groups focus on a single brand of DCC system.

Chapter 3 noted that the rails form a dividing line: The equipment you buy to feed power to the rails should be from the same manufacturer. Exceptions to this are the power supply that plugs in the wall and the circuit breakers or reverse-loop adapters that connect the output of the power booster to the rails, which can be any brand. Also, the decoders themselves can be from any manufacturer.

The comparison table, **1**, lists the features of several DCC systems. As you begin shopping, start by considering the number of operators that will be running trains on your layout. System sizes range from all-in-one units limited to two operators to systems that can handle more than 100.

Does your layout use walkaround control? Even small all-in-one systems have provisions for adding walkaround control, and almost all DCC systems have wireless capability. Also, check that compatible power boosters are available for the system if you expand your layout.

Remember that the signal on the rails is standardized by the National Model Railroad Association (NMRA), but each manufacturer's connection between the command station and the cab or throttle is proprietary, **2**. When you select a system, you're committed to using that brand. You should carefully compare the cabs and throttles of various systems as part of your selection process.

Knobs or buttons

Once you've selected a brand, you need to determine the types and number of cabs (throttles) to match the number of operators running the layout.

There are two basic types of throttles. A full-feature cab with an LCD display and full keypad allows operators to program decoders and run accessory decoders. Smaller cabs with only basic (speed, direction, and limited function) controls are less expensive

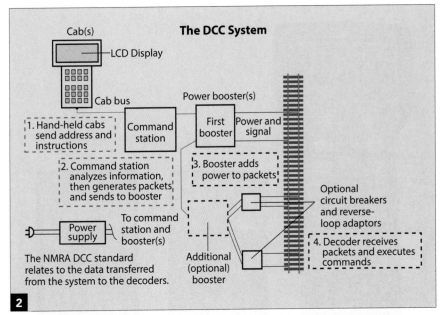

The NMRA DCC standard relates to the data transferred from the system to the decoders.

2

All components of the DCC system itself should come from the same manufacturer. Circuit breakers, reversing modules, and power supplies can be from any maker.

and work best for operators who only run trains.

Many DCC owners buy just one or two full-feature cabs for setting up locomotives and operating accessory decoders, with the rest being limited-feature throttles designed just for running trains.

Cabs use either knobs or keys (push buttons) to control speed. Both work well; the choice is a matter of personal preference.

Some clubs have found it easier on finances to have members buy their own cabs. That allows members to select the type of cab that they prefer, and lets them use the cabs on their home layouts as well.

Function keys

Sound is rapidly gaining in popularity, even in N scale. Be sure the system and cabs you choose have enough function keys to operate the sound features, even if you initially don't use sound.

Some systems provide function keys from F0 to F9, but a better choice is F0 to F12. The increasing number of sounds in newer decoders has put a strain on even 12 keys. Model Rectifier Corp. (MRC) has extended some of its cabs to handle F0 to F19, and the firm's newer sound systems can make use of all of these function keys (the NMRA now has provisions for up to 28 function keys). Many of the newer cabs and throttles use shift keys

3	Typical current loads for HO scale		
Layout item	**Current draw**	**Notes**	
Locomotive (can motor) with sound	0.3A to 0.5A	Newer enclosed or can motor	
Locomotive (open-frame motor)	0.5A to 0.9A	Many pre-1990 models	
Locomotive idle with sound	0.05A	QSI decoder with sound and horn on	
Passenger car with lamps	0.20A to 0.35A	Running current	
Passenger car with LEDs	0.05A	Light bar with seven LEDs	
Switch machine, stall type	0.02A	Constant draw	
Switch machine, twin coil	Up to 3A	Momentary draw only—see note below	

This chart was compiled using actual readings from a RRampMeter. The locomotives were tested under a load. You can make a list and add all devices to determine the requirements for your layout. Locomotives in smaller scales will use less current; in larger scales, more. When running a consist (multiple locomotives), be sure to multiply the current by the number of locomotives in the consist. Twin-coil switch machines are normally powered by capacitor-discharge power supplies. This type of supply only draws current when it recharges and normally at a much lower current.

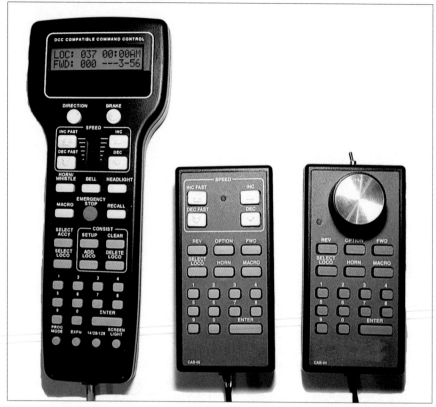

Here are three types of cabs made by NCE. The one on the left has is a full-function cab that can control a system. The other two are operator-only cabs with a choice of push buttons or a knob for speed control. Recently NCE added the Cab 06, which has four digit light-emitting diode display, support for 29 functions, up to 6 recalls, individual accessory control, and macros.

The NCE Twin is a DCC system that works well with an entry-level train set. It can be expanded with walkaround cabs and includes an international power supply.

to allow access to all the increased functions. Another solution is using the same function key for different sounds depending on whether the engine is moving or stopped. For example, on a QSI sound decoder, pressing F7 when moving causes a flange/brake squeal,

and when stopped (neutral) causes a long air let-off.

Wireless cabs

Standard cabs have cables that must be plugged into jacks on the layout. Wireless cabs are more expensive,

but have the advantage of allowing operators to move around without having to plug in their throttles.

As an example, a local narrow gauge modular group originally used tethered cabs on its modular layout. Each trip around the modules required plugging and unplugging the cab at least four times. After upgrading to wireless cabs, members could then walk around the layout without concern for tangled cords or finding an unused plug-in.

Two types of wireless throttles are available: infrared (IR) and radio. Infrared cabs operate like a TV remote control. Operation with IR requires line-of-sight communications with a receiver connected to the network.

Radio cabs are low-power and have a limited roaming range from the base station. Radio can have a problem with "null" spots; just moving a couple of inches normally corrects this problem. People standing in the room can also affect radio transmissions.

Radio cabs use two types of communications: simplex, where the cab sends out the commands and there is no feedback from the command station; or duplex, which uses two-way communications between the command station and the cab.

The NCE radio link is done by an adapter in the cab. A wireless base station is connected to the cab bus. This is a duplex link, with the LCD on the cab updated by the command station. The wireless feature is available on the larger Pro Cab as well as the smaller basic cabs. NCE also has wireless repeaters to increase the useable area.

Digitrax sells the DT400R and UT4R radio throttles. Like most other manufacturers, Digitrax uses simplex transmission. The wireless units also require the UR91 base station, which connects to the LocoNet.

A new item with Digitrax is a Wi-Fi adapter for the LocoNet. (See chapter 12.) Digitrax also makes IR (infrared) cabs and receivers.

CVP, maker of EasyDCC, produces wireless systems, including the ALR900. This system is designed to work with Lenz and Atlas (the latter no longer produced) DCC

The entry-level Digitrax Zephyr is an all-in-one DCC system that includes a power-supply transformer. The new Zephyr Xtra has a 3-amp output. A LocoNet connection allows walkaround cabs to be used. The Zephyr Xtra can also be programmed to operate as a booster. This is a handy feature when you expand your layout and add DCC devices. *Digitrax*

Cabs come in a variety of styles and configurations. These are the MRC Prodigy Express cab, NCE ProCab, NCE Cab-04, Digitrax UT4, and Digitrax DT400. Some manufacturers call them cabs and some call them throttles.

The MRC Prodigy Express includes a plug-in power supply, the command station, and the handheld cab. The system shown here can easily be upgraded by plugging a Prodigy Advance cab into the throttle bus.

systems, a rare case of commonality between manufacturers on the "below-rail" side.

CVP also makes the CONVRTR. The small circuit board (.8" x 2.0") connects to any DCC decoder and a 12 volt battery, all of which fits into a locomotive. The CVP AirWire900 handheld throttle communicates directly with the circuit board. This combination lets you run a locomotive without power on the rails.

Lenz has two ways of using wireless cabs. One way of establishing a radio link between the cab and command station uses a standard off-the-shelf cordless telephone to transmit commands. Any cordless-phone base station can be connected to the Lenz XPA or XpressNet tone adaptor. The adaptor uses the familiar DTMF (dual tone multi frequency) tones generated by the phone for communicating digital information. Lenz also has an adapter that uses smart phones and Wi-Fi to connect to the XpressNet.

Although radio reception generally isn't a problem in most layout rooms, wireless cabs perform best when in line-of-sight with the antenna. The center of the layout on the ceiling is a good location for the antenna. The wireless adapter should be installed so the operator's normal position isn't between the radio and cab. Repeater stations are available that can help with wireless signal coverage.

Fast clock

Another feature of many DCC systems is a fast clock with an adjustable time ratio. The clock can be set so you can have an operating session covering a 12- to 24-hour period in one evening. The fast clock time can be shown in the display of some cabs.

Command station

Regardless of size, a model railroad uses only a single DCC command station, which with some systems is combined with a power booster. This is the way all-in-one systems work.

The command station provides power to the cabs and data to the boosters. This can be in the form of a single bus like Digitrax's LocoNet, which connects to both the throttles and the power boosters, or separate connections like the NCE cab bus and control bus (for power boosters).

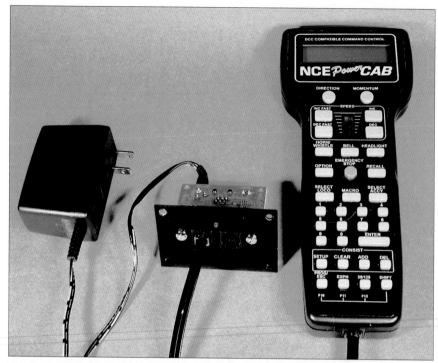

The Power Cab is NCE's all-in-one handheld cab with a built-in command station and booster. The Power Cab will operate as a normal cab when used with other NCE systems.

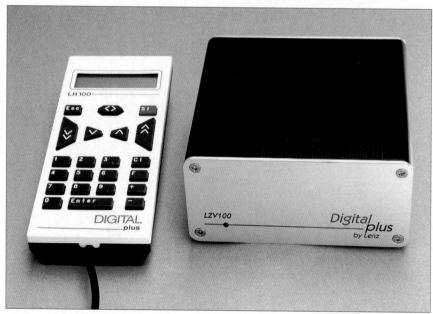

The Lenz system comes with either an LH100 push button cab or LH90 knob-style cab. For wireless operation, Lenz has an adapter that uses a standard cordless telephone. The LH100 and the command station with booster (right) is the Set100.

ECoS

The ECoS system from ESU has unique features that put it in a class by itself. The system uses a 7" touchscreen to set up and control locomotives and accessories. The unit is like a PC and boots up each time it is powered on. The program that operates the ECoS runs a version of Linux.

There are two controls, one on each side of the unit. When you use the touchscreen to set speed, the motor-driven knob moves to match the screen. When you enter locomotive information, a typewriter-style keyboard comes up on the touchscreen,

and you can enter information using your finger or the provided stylus. Once entered, the system retains the data, allowing you to easily select a locomotive from the list.

ECoS not only supports DCC, but also the Motorola, Selectrix, and LGB formats. Wireless cabs are being planned, and there's an Ethernet connection for use with a computer.

One of the system's most interesting features is the ability to connect any DCC system to an input on the ECoS. As a test, I connected my NCE system to the ECoS. After linking the address of the locomotive that I wanted to run to the ECoS data file, I could run the locomotive using either the NCE system or the ECoS unit. Since the input commands are at the DCC rail level, any DCC-compatible system should work. You can even run with the added DCC system's wireless control.

The ECoS system includes an 18-volt transformer, which can be exchanged for a 15-volt transformer for use with N and Z scales.

Power boosters

Each DCC system comes with a power booster, which is adequate for most small layouts. Additional power boosters are needed when current needs exceed what the original booster can supply. Boosters have ratings from 2 to 10 amps. Smaller DCC starter systems have low ratings, like the Digitrax Zephyr Xtra (3A) and the NCE Power Cab and Twin (2A). When adding extra boosters, be sure they're compatible with your command station. The power from one booster is called a booster district; adapters can be added to create power districts so a single short will not shut the entire layout down.

Model Rectifier Corp.'s new Prodigy Elite is rated at 10 amps, which is suitable for O scale and large scale. You normally shouldn't use this much power for smaller scales. The output current on the Elite is adjustable for use with smaller scales.

How much power?

Determine how much current each of your locomotives draw, **3**. A rough

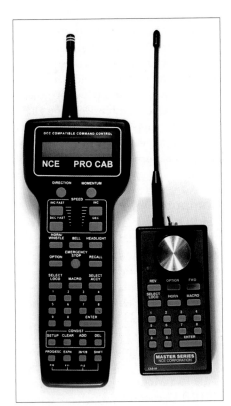

NCE's wireless cabs use external antennas. Two lengths of antennas are available, short and long. Some modelers have replaced the external antenna with a short length of flexible wire or a Splatch internal antenna.

estimate is about 2 amps for G scale, 1.5 amps for O, 1 amp for S, .75 amps for HO, and .5 amps for N. For narrow gauge, just drop down one scale.

Older open-frame motors will draw more current; newer enclosed motors (standard in most mid- to high-end locomotives since the 1990s) draw significantly less. Some sound-equipped locomotives will draw almost double the amount of current of a non-sound model.

Accessory decoders that drive devices like stall-motor switch machines and other accessories add to the power requirement. For example, a Tortoise (Circuitron) switch motor draws 20 milliamps (.020A) when stalled, so 50 Tortoises would require 1 amp. If you have a lot of accessory decoders, consider using a separate booster just for them.

To calculate the total current draw for the layout, start with the total number of operators (trains), add any extra consisted engines, then multiply

The SB5 is NCE's new 5-amp Smart Booster used with the PowerCab. It allows the PowerCab to be disconnected and moved. *NCE*

This is the 5-amp booster used with NCE's SB5. It comes with international power supply. *NCE*

by the current draw per engine for your scale—being sure to account for any sound-equipped models.

Add current draw for any passenger car lights, and you have an approximate current requirement for your layout. You may find that a single booster is all that is needed. More boosters can be added later if the current limit of the original booster is exceeded.

The common booster rating is five amps. This will work for most scales. Ten-amp boosters are also available, but these should be reserved for

scales larger than HO. With 10 amps available, the rail resistance on HO and N scale layouts might not be low enough to trip the booster's circuit breaker when a short occurs. A short-circuit with 10 amps can do serious damage and possibly cause components to overheat or even melt.

Power supply

Most systems require a separate power supply. There are a number of transformers designed for use with DCC systems, but transformers don't

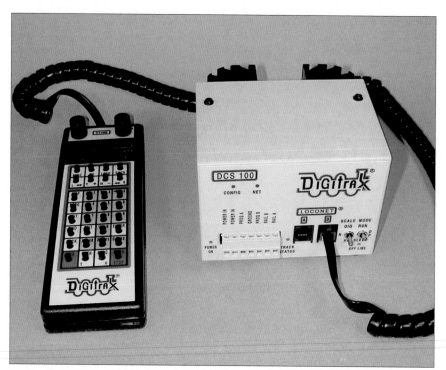

This is the Digitrax DC100 set, with a combined command station and booster (right). The UT400 cab (left) is Digitrax's top-of-the-line unit, and is also available in a wireless (radio) version.

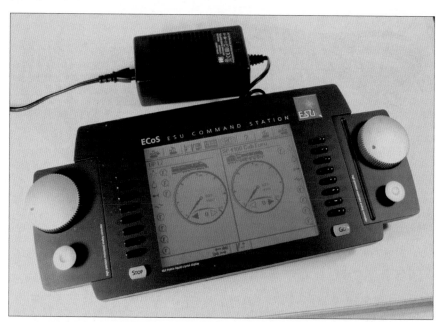

The ECoS system by ESU has several unique features, including a 7" touch screen and the ability to function as a bridge between the rails and another DCC system.

of short circuits between boosters and common transformers. It also makes troubleshooting easier. A transformer with a power switch is handy; if it doesn't have one, use a power strip with a switch and circuit breaker. Plug all your power supplies into a single power strip. This allows power for the entire layout to be turned off with a single switch.

Computer interface
Most DCC systems can be connected to a PC or Macintosh using the USB serial port as an interface; the ECoS system uses an Ethernet connection. Some older systems use the RS232 serial port—adapters (with and without cords) are available to connect an RS232 to a USB port.

Programs are available to do a number of different tasks. One example is the Java Model Railroad Interface (JMRI) DecoderPro, which programs decoders and then remembers the settings of the decoders' CVs. This makes it easy to refresh a decoder if it gets "amnesia." (More on JMRI in Chapter 12.)

You can also use on-screen control panels to operate turnouts with a mouse. This makes setting up a Centralized Traffic Control (CTC) operation a lot easier than wiring all of the switch machines to a control panel. With the coming of DCC bidirectional data, the control panel could also show the location of each locomotive.

Decoders
Any brand of decoder should work with any DCC system, so selecting a locomotive decoder depends on your scale (the decoder must fit in your model), the current draw of your locomotive (the decoder power rating must be high enough), and your preference of sound effects (the latest sound decoders provide a wide range of engine sounds to match specific prototype steam and diesel locomotives).

To find more information on specific decoders, see their instruction manuals—most of which can be downloaded from manufacturers' Websites.

need to be from the same manufacturer as your DCC system. Some systems, including the Digitrax Zephyr, ESU ECoS, NCE Power Cab, and MRC Prodigy, include a power supply.

The command station and first booster are normally combined into one unit and powered by a single transformer. Adding more boosters

means adding more input power. The easiest way to do this is to use a separate transformer for each added booster. The transformer should have a current rating slightly higher than the rated output of the booster. Most use 15- to 18-volt transformers.

Using a separate transformer for each booster eliminates the possibility

CHAPTER SEVEN

Wiring a layout for DCC

Building a new DCC-controlled layout or converting an older layout to DCC both require planning the wiring. In the early days of DCC, some suggested the process of wiring was simply connecting two wires to the rails. Another article on converting a layout to DCC began by removing all DC wiring and rewiring the whole layout. In most cases the answer lies between those two extremes.

Organizing your wiring, providing adequate power, dividing your layout into power districts, and providing convenient sockets for plug-in throttles will help you get the most out of a DCC-equipped layout. *David Popp*

Throttle panels allow operators to quickly connect and disconnect throttles. Place these every few feet along the fascia and at busy locations of the layout. You may not need as many of these panels if you're running wireless. Even with wireless control a few panels are needed when operators are out of range or when batteries run low.

Connecting just two wires to the rails severely limits DCC flexibility, but ripping out all existing wiring and starting over may be a waste of time and money.

Making the switch

When converting from DC to DCC there are some wiring considerations to think about. With DCC you can have one or more locomotives (including those equipped with sound) operating in a block. Even switch machines may be operating off track power. With DC you're limited to just the locomotive you're running.

About the time the first edition of this book came out, Jim Betz and I converted a medium-size double-deck layout from DC to DCC. In this case, the original wiring was marginally acceptable, so we replaced all of it. Replacing the wire with a heavier gauge and adding feeder wires from the rails made a big improvement, resulting in smooth DCC operation.

Ways to wire

No two layouts are the same, and DCC requirements vary with each one. Consider the scale and the number of operators when converting a DC layout or building a new model railroad.

A small layout with one operator may get away with only the two-wires-to-the-rails solution. A club or home layout with several operators and lots of trains needs to be divided into several

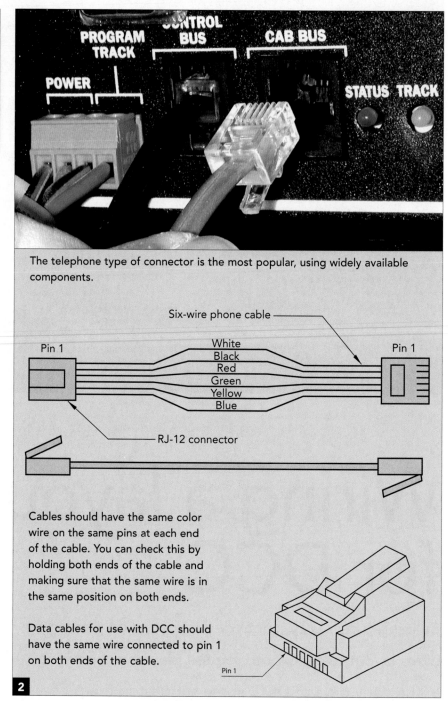

The telephone type of connector is the most popular, using widely available components.

Cables should have the same color wire on the same pins at each end of the cable. You can check this by holding both ends of the cable and making sure that the same wire is in the same position on both ends.

Data cables for use with DCC should have the same wire connected to pin 1 on both ends of the cable.

electrical blocks or districts to prevent a single short circuit or overload from shutting down the entire layout.

I began converting my layout from cab control to DCC by connecting the DCC system in place of one of my DC power packs. This provided the ability to operate on DCC, but still allowed DC operation. It gave me a chance to install decoders as time and money become available. However, trying to run DC and DCC on the same layout at the same time isn't recommended.

Cab wiring

Walkaround ability is part of every DCC system. Handheld cabs need power and a way to communicate with the command station.

Cabs are either tethered or wireless. Tethered cabs require plug-in connections placed in convenient locations around the layout, **1**. The connections should be near areas of rail activity, such as yards, industrial areas, towns, and passing sidings. On multi-deck layouts, the plug-in connections

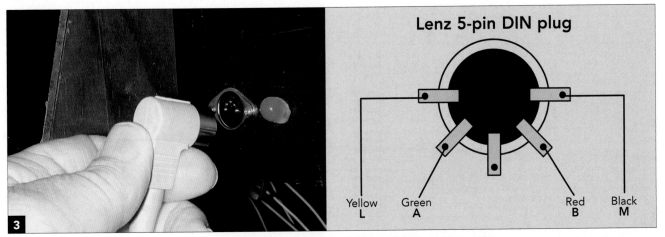

Lenz 5-pin DIN plug

Yellow
L
Green
A
Red
B
Black
M

3

Lenz uses a five-wire DIN-style connector. The diagram shows the wiring used for Lenz XpressNet.

4	**Pin-connector references**				
Pin no.	Wire color	NCE Cab Bus	Digitrax LocoNet	Lenz Xpress Net	Lenz DIN 5
1	White	No connection (reversed)	Rail Sync	No connection	
2	Black	Ground	Ground	Ground	"M"
3	Red	-RS-485	LocoNet	-RS-485	"B"
4	Green	+RS-485	LocoNet	+RS-485	"A"
5	Yellow	+12 volts	Ground	+12 volts	"L"
6	Blue	No connection (reversed)	Rail Sync	No connection	

are only needed on the lower level.

Even with the freedom of wireless control, it's important to have a few plug-in connections around the layout for use when wireless cab batteries are low or you are in a dead radio spot or out of wireless range. You may also find that acquiring a locomotive, programming it, and building a consist go faster if the cab is plugged in.

Connectors for tethered cabs vary among systems. The telephone-style RJ12 (four- and six-pin) is the most popular type, **2**, allowing operators to quickly plug and unplug their cab when moving to different locations. Some exceptions include MRC, which uses an eight-pin phone connector. Lenz uses the DIN-5 connector, **3**.

Check your system's manual regarding routing cab wiring. Most require cab panels to be "daisy chained," or wired from one connector to the next. Branching out or looping back to the source may not be allowed. You can use standard telephone wire for short runs or small to medium-size layouts. For long runs or large layouts where noise pickup is suspected of causing interference with signals between cabs and the command station, use Category 5 (Cat-5) cable. This cable has shielded wire, which reduces interference from rail power. The chart in **4** shows the function of each wire for various manufacturers' systems.

Most telephone-style connectors for DCC are wired as data cables, with pin 1 to pin 1. An exception is CVP, which uses the phone-type connection of pin 1 to pin 6.

You can purchase ready-to-use phone and data cables, or make your own using separate connectors and a crimper, **5**. This is also handy for repairing broken connectors.

Two-wire vs. common rail

There are two methods of wiring a layout, two-rail wiring and common-rail wiring, **6**.

Two-rail wiring is the most popular and easiest to understand. As its name implies, two-rail wiring uses two wires from the power source to the rails. The layout is divided into blocks, with two wires (from a booster or circuit breaker in DCC or from a block-control toggle switch in DC) going to each block.

With common-rail wiring, only one rail is divided into blocks (other than reversing blocks.) The other rail is continuous, providing a common electrical return for all blocks. Common-rail wiring doesn't work well with multiple boosters, and it's generally best to avoid it for DCC.

In both types of wiring, circuit protection is needed to protect the

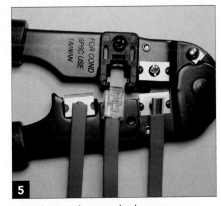

5

The plastic tabs on telephone-type connectors sometimes break, but a crimping tool makes the connectors easy to replace. You can also use the crimper to make new cables. Use a good-quality crimping tool – cheap crimpers make cheap connections!

power source from overloads and short circuits.

DC, DCC power differences

On a DC cab-control layout, each operator has a power pack, with toggle or rotary switches routing the power from each operator's pack to specific blocks as a train moves around the

DCC two-rail wiring

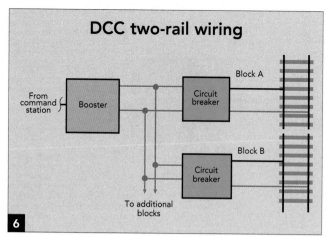

There are two choices for wiring a layout. Common-rail wiring can cut down the number of wires, but can be a little confusing. It's recommended for layouts with two or more boosters. Two-rail wiring (shown here) is easier to understand and the more popular method.

Short circuit on cab-control DC layout

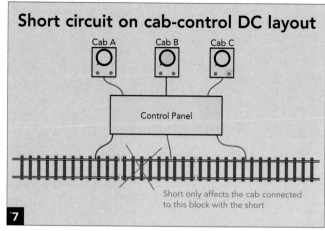

Short only affects the cab connected to this block with the short

Short circuits on DC layouts only affect the train in the block with the short. When a short occurs on a layout with DCC, the booster shuts down, killing power to the entire layout. Adding more blocks and circuit breakers limits the areas affected by short circuits.

Medium-size DCC layout

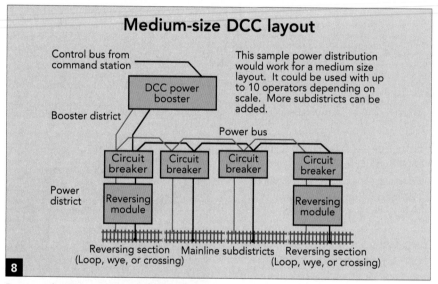

This sample power distribution would work for a medium size layout. It could be used with up to 10 operators depending on scale. More subdistricts can be added.

Reversing section (Loop, wye, or crossing)   Mainline subdistricts   Reversing section (Loop, wye, or crossing)

Booster districts can be divided into power districts by adding circuit breakers between the booster and sections of the main line.

layout. When a short circuit occurs, only the operator running the involved train is affected, **7**. Other trains continue to run because they are controlled by separate power packs.

With DCC, the power to the rails comes from a booster that's fed instructions from a command station. These instructions come from each operator's cab. On a layout with a single power booster and no other circuit protection, a short circuit will shut down the entire layout, stopping all trains.

The DC cab-control method of separating track into blocks, with circuit protection for each block, can be used on a DCC layout to minimize the effects of short circuits.

This is like a house wired with a main circuit breaker that shuts off all the power, followed by several secondary circuit breakers or fuses used for smaller areas of the home, **8**. If the total amount of power used in a home exceeds the rating of the main breaker, it will trip; otherwise, overloads and shorts only affect their respective circuits.

DCC power boosters have their own built-in circuit breakers that are like the main breaker in a home. Additional breakers can be added between the booster and track.

Blocks for DCC

Dividing a layout into blocks for DCC can be done in much the same way as DC. The difference is that more than one train can be running independently in a block. Also, blocks can be longer, so you'll usually wind up with fewer blocks in DCC. This results in more locomotives in a single, longer electrical block. You may need to wire these blocks with heavier wire.

Blocks fed by a booster are booster districts; blocks feed from circuit breakers connected to boosters are power districts. Decide where to place block boundaries based on the probability of where short circuits will occur. Yards, industrial areas, and branch lines are good candidates for separate power. Sections of main line with passing sidings or crossovers are another. You can always divide power districts into smaller blocks later if needed.

When making a booster district or power district, the rails must be gapped to electrically isolate the district's rails.

My DC layout had 16 blocks on the main line (including two reverse loops) plus another four for yards and branch lines for a total of 20 blocks.

With DCC, my layout now has ten power districts. The main line is now protected by six circuit breakers, **9**. Two of the six mainline blocks are reverse loops and use reverse loop adapters that include circuit breakers.

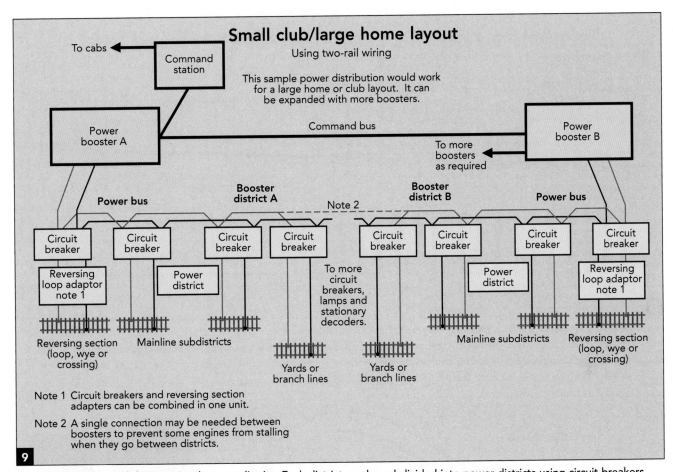

Small club/large home layout
Using two-rail wiring

This sample power distribution would work for a large home or club layout. It can be expanded with more boosters.

To cabs

Command station

Power booster A

Command bus

To more boosters as required

Power booster B

Power bus

Booster district A

Note 2

Booster district B

Power bus

Circuit breaker (×8)

Reversing loop adaptor note 1

Power district

To more circuit breakers, lamps and stationary decoders.

Power district

Reversing loop adaptor note 1

Reversing section (loop, wye or crossing)

Mainline subdistricts

Yards or branch lines

Yards or branch lines

Mainline subdistricts

Reversing section (loop, wye or crossing)

Note 1 Circuit breakers and reversing section adapters can be combined in one unit.

Note 2 A single connection may be needed between boosters to prevent some engines from stalling when they go between districts.

9

Track powered by each booster is a booster district. Each district can be subdivided into power districts using circuit breakers. Additional boosters can be added for larger layouts.

Power districts

More power districts and boosters are needed when you have exceeded the power of the existing booster(s). When more than one power district is used, the DCC signal in each district must be in phase with the adjacent district, meaning the polarity of the rails at the gapped joint between districts must match. If the polarity doesn't match, a locomotive passing over the border will cause a short circuit as its metal wheels bridge the gap.

There can also be a problem with some engines stalling halfway across the gaps. Modern models with all-wheel electrical pickup won't have this problem, but some older locomotives have electrical pickup staggered between trucks (or the drivers and tender) so that the left-rail pickup is on one side of the gap and the right-rail pickup is on the other. Check your system manual for any special instructions on connecting boosters together.

Power district protection

Booster districts can be further divided into power districts so a single short will not shut down the whole booster district. Power districts are less expensive to add than boosters. Each block should have individual circuit protection. Power districts are protected with circuit breakers, **9**. Don't use fuses, as they'll have to be replaced each time a short occurs.

The circuit breaker should be rated or set to trip at a current less than the output of the booster. Circuit breakers also must cut the current off in less time than the booster's built-in breaker (some circuit breakers have adjustable timing). Some circuit breakers have special settings to work with entry-level systems. Circuit breakers designed to work with DCC automatically reset themselves about once per second until the short is cleared.

Some circuit breakers have an output to feed an LED to show when the breaker is tripped and power is

10

The circuit board on the left is a Power Shield (PSX-1) single circuit breaker. The circuit board on the right is a PSX-AR reversing module with circuit breaker. These solid-state circuit breakers are designed to sense the difference between a short circuit and the high inrush current used to charge capacitors.

off. Some manufacturers include more than one breaker in a single unit. These circuit breakers can be driven by a single booster.

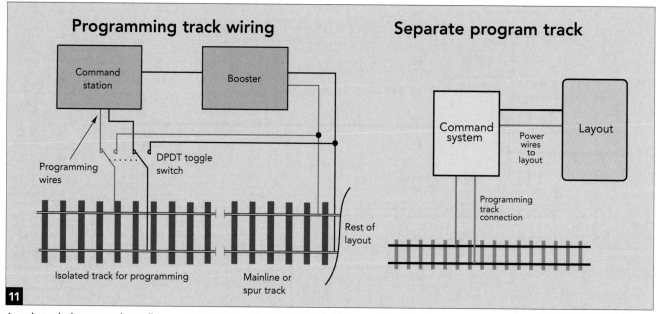

Programming track wiring

Command station

Booster

Programming wires

DPDT toggle switch

Isolated track for programming

Mainline or spur track

Rest of layout

Separate program track

Command system

Power wires to layout

Layout

Programming track connection

11

A stub-ended spur works well as a programming track (Left). A double-pole double-throw center-off toggle allows switching the track from programming to layout power. Another choice is to use a separate piece of track not connected to the layout. This eliminates the possible problem of wheels shorting between the program track and the main line. A section of track, like flex track, as a handier place to connect to the programming track (right).

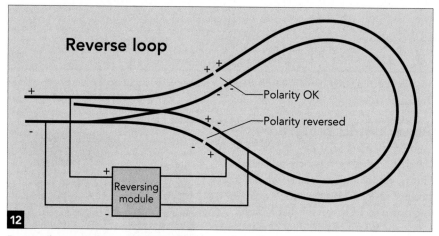

Reverse loop

Polarity OK

Polarity reversed

Reversing module

12

Reverse loop adapters automatically change the polarity of the isolated reversing track section as the train enters or leaves the section.

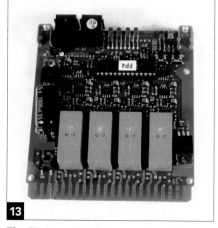

13

The Digitrax PM42 is a combination circuit breaker/reverse loop adapter. Each of its four sections can be assigned for either function with an adjustable trip current of 1.5 to 12 amps.

Sound decoders and circuit breakers

When a circuit breaker trips due to a short circuit, it removes power to that power district. This causes a problem with some newer sound decoders, which have large capacitors that must be charged after power is removed. This power surge can be enough for a circuit breaker to see it as a short circuit and trip again. Sometimes it takes multiple sound-equipped locomotives operating at once to cause this to happen.

One solution is to add more power districts and circuit breakers so there

won't be as many locomotives in a block. Some newer circuit breakers are designed to solve this problem.

The Power Shield X series from DCC Specialties solves the capacitor overload problem by using a microprocessor to determine if a power surge is a short or just discharged capacitors, **10**.

Another circuit breaker is the NCE EB1. The amperage ratings of these breakers is adjustable. Strings of passenger cars with interior lights can also cause overloads. Converting car lighting from lamps to LEDs can resolve this problem.

Programming track

The programming track, an isolated section of track used for programming decoders, is fed by two dedicated wires from the command station. The current to the programming track is limited, so a decoder can be tested without damaging it if there's a short circuit in the locomotive wiring. A dead-end spur within easy reach of the side of the layout is a good choice for the programming track, **11**, with insulated gaps in both rails to isolate the track.

This PSX reversing loop adapter is wired to a helix. Neat wiring makes it easy to troubleshoot. *Vince Vargus*

(You can also use a piece of track separate from your layout, perhaps on your workbench.)

If your programming track is on your layout, use a double-pole, double throw (DPDT) center-off toggle switch to change the rails from normal to programming track operation. The center-off feature allows track power to be turned off while placing equipment on it, avoiding short circuits.

When programming a locomotive, be sure the wheels of any equipment on the programming track don't bridge the gaps to the rest of the layout.

Some DCC systems leave track power on when in programming track mode (Digitrax, MRC, ECoS); some turn off the main line power (Lenz, NCE). To be on the safe side, program decoders on a separate section of track to prevent the locomotive's wheels from bridging the gap.

Reversing sections and loops

Any section of track where a train can reverse its direction of travel on the layout is a reversing section. Reverse loops are the most common type; wyes and turntables also qualify.

When wiring reversing tracks, the isolated section of track for the reversing section must be longer than the longest train that will use it, and both rails must be electrically isolated from the rest of the layout.

In wiring reverse loops on a standard DC layout, you typically reverse the polarity of the main line before the train exits the reversing section.

With DCC, you leave the mainline polarity alone and reverse the polarity

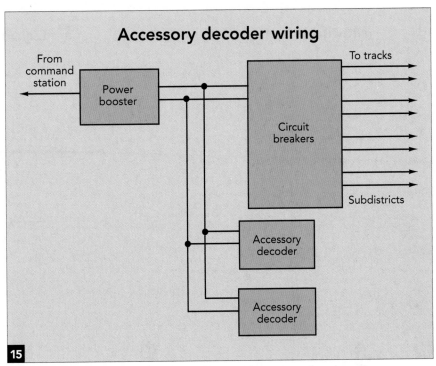

Using a separate booster for the accessories and stationary decoders allows a turnout to operate when there is a short circuit in the block with the turnout.

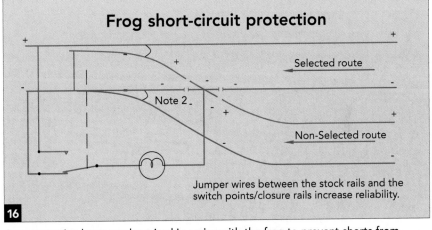

An automotive lamp can be wired in series with the frog to prevent shorts from tripping the circuit breaker or booster. A no. 1156 auto lamp works for HO and larger scales when using at least a 5-amp booster. The nos. 912 or 1141 lamps can be used for smaller scales and boosters with less power.

of the reversing section when the train is entering or exiting reversing section. This is possible in DCC because the decoder, not the track polarity, controls the locomotive's direction.

The polarity of the reversing section can be changed with switch machine contacts or a toggle switch, but the best way is with a DCC reversing module, **12**.

DCC reversing modules, **13** (and **10**), are connected between the power source and the rails in the reversing

section. As a train either enters or exits the loop, a short circuit will occur. The reverse loop adapter senses the short and flips the polarity of the reversing section before the booster senses the short and shuts down. This allows the train to continue without any action by the operator.

Both electro-mechanical and electronic reverse loop adapters are available. One electronic adapter, the PSX-AR (**14**), includes an output that operates a turnout as the train goes

Modified turnout

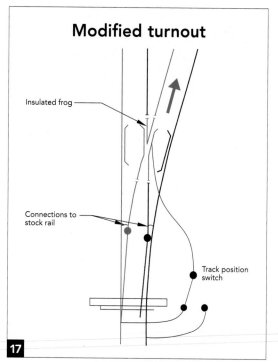

Insulated frog

Connections to stock rail

Track position switch

17

Turnouts can be wired to reduce the chances of a metal wheel causing a short circuit between the stock and point rails.

Layout organization

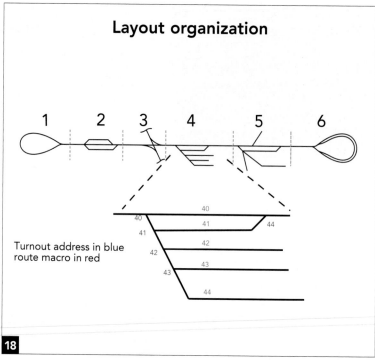

1   2   3   4   5   6

Turnout address in blue route macro in red

40
40   41   44
41
42   42
43   43
44

18

This is a sample of how portions of a layout could be logically numbered.

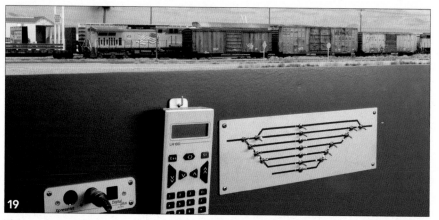

19

This yard control panel is on Pelle Soeborg's HO layout. The switch panel graphics can include numbers for operating turnouts remotely with DCC. The cab and plug panel are from Lenz.

through a loop, essentially automating the reverse loop. The MRC and Digitrax reverse loop adapters are electro-mechanical. The electronic reverser switches in microseconds, the relay type in milliseconds. The momentary delay with relays can cause a slight hesitation when it switches polarity. The faster the reverser switches, the smoother the train operation.

Accessory decoders

Accessory decoders can be powered by connecting them to the rails.

However, if you've wired a layout with circuit breakers, it's better to power accessory decoders directly from the booster, bypassing the circuit breakers. This way a short will not affect the accessory decoders.

For large layouts, consider powering accessory decoders with a separate power booster, **15**. This solves the problem of a train entering the non-selected route of a turnout, which shorts out the block and cuts off the power to the accessory decoder, so the turnout can't be changed to clear the

short! Normally a 3 amp booster is sufficient.

Turnouts

One common cause of short circuits is a train entering the frog end of a turnout with the points set the wrong way.

One fix to keep the power from shutting down is to wire an auto lamp in series with the frog so only the lamp will light on a short, **16**. Another way is to have the turnout automatically aligned with an accessory decoder like the Hare or the Wabbit from DCC Specialities with a Tortoise by Circuitron switch motor. Another cure for this problem is Tam Valley Depot's Frog Juicer. The device switches the power source faster than the circuit breaker can trip.

Metal wheels can sometimes cause short circuits when going through a turnout. This is usually the fault of a wheelset being too wide or narrow in gauge. If this happens, check the wheelset with an NMRA standards gauge and fix or replace it if needed.

These shorts can also be the fault of the turnout if the gauge is too tight at the points or frog. Again, check the

20 Length in feet for ½ volt drop				
Wire size	1 amp	2 amps	5 amps	10 amps
8	796	398	59	80
10	50	250	100	50
12	314	157	63	31
14	198	99	40	20
16	124	62	25	12
18	78	39	16	8
20	50	25	10	5

This chart lists wire lengths for a .5-volt drop for a single one-way run of wire. Double it for a pair of wires feeding a block from the source.

You can measure the loss in voltage with a voltmeter while current is flowing. The RRampMeter reads both volts (RMS) and current. The load should be about equal to the normal load in the block or district. The photo shows a lamp that drew .76 amps at 13 volts, about the right current for an HO power district.

turnout with an NMRA gauge, and fix or replace the turnout if needed. A quick fix is to give the frog a coat of clear fingernail polish. This will insulate the frog and keep metal wheels from shorting against it.

To minimize shorts caused by metal wheels and to increase reliability, turnouts can be wired with insulated switch rods and the points electrically connected to the stock rail, **17**. Using the rail points as an electrical switch is a source of intermittent problems. They may cause shorts or not make contact. New layouts should use non-power-routing turnouts, such as those labeled the "DCC friendly." Locomotives with super capacitors can run through dead turnouts without stalling.

Layout organization

Blocks and districts should be identified with a number or name. Some layout owners name their districts alphabetically (Allentown, Bakersfield, Campbell, and so on). I find using numbers works better because you can group switch machine addresses to match.

A layout needs some form of identification of blocks and districts. It can either be by number or name. Some have named their districts alphabetically by name like and so on. Using numbers works better because you can also group switch machine addresses to match, **18**. For example, in district 4, switch machines could have addresses of 40 to 49. If there are more than 10 addresses, the run could start at 400. This numbering could also be applied to the circuit breakers and block detectors in a district. Control panels can also be used to show switch numbers, **19**.

Terminal strips and other devices under the layout also need identification. Whether it's you or somebody else working on the wiring, it's a lot easier to trace a problem when you have the wiring clearly identified. When installing terminal strips and circuit beakers, it's easy to write the device's ID nearby.

All layout wiring information should be kept in a file or binder for future reference. Be sure to update the information as you make changes.

Voltage drop and signal loss

You'll need fairly heavy wire to carry the track power around the layout, with regularly spaced track feeders to the rails. One feeder for each flextrack-length rail is ideal – about every three feet.

The chart in **20** shows the voltage drop for various wire sizes depending upon the amperage carried. The higher

Tony's Train Exchange sells the RRamp Meter. This device measures a DCC system's output. *Adrian Pardo*

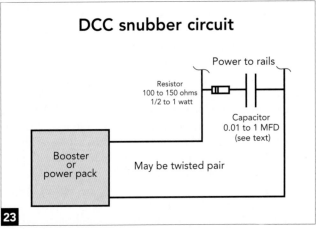

DCC snubber circuit

Power to rails

Resistor
100 to 150 ohms
1/2 to 1 watt

Capacitor
0.01 to 1 MFD
(see text)

Booster
or
power pack

May be twisted pair

A snubber can help minimize the distortion of the DCC signal over long wire runs.

Though careful planning is an important part of any great model railroad, extra planning is necessary when installing DCC on a large layout. Here are stories from two 1,200-square-foot multi-level layouts.

David Parks' double-deck Cumberland Western layout features the Baltimore & Ohio and Western Maryland. The two railroads are independent of each other, requiring separate DCC systems with the boosters side by side.

Though having the boosters in one location seemed like a good idea, there were some problems in the blocks with the longer power cables. The fix was to shorten the cables by moving the boosters closer to the blocks, reducing the cable length by half. Most of the problems disappeared. David

stated that if he were to do it over again, he'd distribute the boosters around the layout closer to the blocks they power.

The Tri-City Society of Model Engineers has a triple-deck layout that depicts the Southern Pacific and Western Pacific in the San Francisco Bay and Niles Canyon areas. Two-thirds of the layout is visible, with the remaining one-third underneath a staging yard that serves both railroads.

The two railroads are independent of each other, also requiring separate DCC systems.

There will be four DCC drawers distributed around the model railroad that slide out from under the layout to allow easy servicing as required.—Don Fiehmann

Though David Parks thought having all of the boosters in one location was a good idea, there were problems in the blocks with longer power cables. He moved the boosters closer to the blocks they power, reducing the cable length by half. This eliminated most of the problems.

The Tri-City Society of Model Engineers model railroad will feature four DCC drawers that slide out from under the layout for easy servicing. *Mark Gurries (two photos)*

---

the current, the greater the voltage drop. Try to keep the voltage loss under 1 volt, or better yet, .5 volt.

If the voltage drop is too great, locomotives will slow down and/or the booster may not sense a short circuit.

Another concern is the DCC signal itself. On a DC layout, the concern on long runs is the resistance of the wire. With DCC, the high-frequency nature of the signal can cause some signal distortion at the end of a long run. For runs longer than 25 feet, twisting the two bus wires together two or three turns per foot can help.

Layout voltage loss should be measured with a load. An automotive lamp with clip leads attached can be used as a load, **21**. Make two measurements, first with no load and then with a load. The difference is the voltage loss.

For accurate readings of DCC power and voltage, use a true RMS meter like the RRampMeter from Tony's Train Exchange, **22**.

Layout wire and connections

For most layouts, 14-gauge wire is adequate, but for large home or club layouts, 12-gauge wire might be necessary. Rail feeders can be much smaller (20- to 22-gauge) since they're shorter and carry less current. Most hardware stores carry heavy gauge solid wire for use in home wiring; RadioShack and hobby shops have smaller gauge wire.

High-current twin-coil type switch machines normally require 14- to 18-gauge bus wires. The new stall-type motors like the Tortoise by Circuitron can use 20- to 24-gauge wires.

With DCC the waveform is a complex square wave as shown in Chapter 3. The signal transition from the minus to positive or back is only a few microseconds. Long cable runs can distort the waveform. An average home layout shouldn't have problems with distorted waveforms. But when the cable runs are longer than 25 feet, the DCC waveform can be distorted,

leading to unresponsive controllers and runaway locomotives.

Installing a snubber at the end of the feeder cable near the rails can help resolve this problem. A snubber is a simple resistor capacitor (R/C) filter network that's installed across the track power near the end of the run at the rails, **23**. If the sunbber doesn't correct the problem, move the booster closer to the districts and power district and use a shorter power cable.

Block detection may pick up the small amount of current used by the snubber. This can be remedied by installing the snubber between the booster and detector near the detector end of the wiring. The following website has more information: sites.google.com/site/markgurries/home/technical-discussions/wiring-planing/snubbers-rc-filter

Solid connections

Make sure wire joints are solid. Crimp-on connectors and soldering both work well if done correctly. When using crimp connectors, be sure to use the connector designed for the wire size you're using, and use a crimping tool designed for that type of connector. When soldering, be sure to get the wire hot enough that the wire (and not the iron) melts the solder.

There have been a number of comments on the Yahoo! groups about soldering two rail sections together. The general consensus is that soldering rails on straight sections can cause problems due to expansion and contraction. Rails on curves is a different matter. Soldering here is critical to rail alignment.

Block detection

Prototype railroad signaling systems detect trains electrically. Low voltage applied to the rails is short-circuited by the trains' steel wheels and axles, indicating their presence in a block. Likewise, the most reliable way to locate trains on a model railroad is by detecting the current flowing to each block.

Many DCC block detectors have what's called a "tombstone," which acts like a transformer, **24**. Running a feeder wire through the hole in the tombstone enables it to detect the current flowing through the wire. This way the detector is isolated from the DCC power, and there's no voltage drop between the power source and the rails.

Another type of detector is DCC Specialties' Block Watcher, which has a low voltage drop with high current. The Block Watcher is addressable with a DCC system. The DCC power is isolated from the detector output.

Other detectors measure the voltage drop across a diode or resistor. These types of detectors aren't always isolated from the DCC power.

Wheelsets are available with a resistor between the two wheels to allow some current to flow for detection. Lamps in passenger cars and cabooses also draw current that can be detected.

The quarter trick

A good way to test existing layout wiring is the popular "quarter trick."

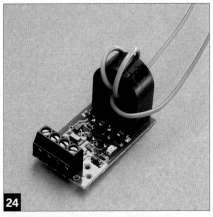

This NCE block-occupancy detector uses transformer action for detection. The block feed wire runs through the black "tombstone" on the circuit board. More turns through the block increase its sensitivity.

Place a quarter or other metal coin across the rails to short-circuit the system. The system should detect a short. If it doesn't, investigate the reason. Undersized bus or feeder wires, excessive rail resistance, and too-few feeders can provide enough resistance that the booster or circuit breaker will not sense a short circuit.

The test should repeated on rails about every 3 feet. It's especially important to do this test at the ends of your power bus runs.

DCC system testing

An inexpensive way to analyze DCC data is with Pricom's DCC Pocket Tester, **25**. This handheld unit analyzes DCC data directly from the rails and is powered by the DCC signal.

Several scroll-through screens let you analyze the DCC data down to the bit level to give you the tolerance of both the one and zero bits. It shows track voltage and can tell you the maximum average and minimum number of preamble bits. You can also see the last 32 locomotives that have been addressed. Select one of the locomotive addresses, and the screen fills with all of the data from the packets for that address. Speed and functions are shown, and operations-mode commands and accessory decoder commands can be seen.

NCE has a DCC Packet Analyzer that connects to a PC or Mac. It uses

The DCC Pocket Tester from Pricom analyzes DCC data directly from the rails.

the RS232 interface and requires a terminal program capable of 38.4 Kbps and 7 bit.

These tools may not be something that everyone needs. A club, large layout, or someone interested in DCC will find these handy tools for analyzing the DCC system. You can also share tools among fellow DCC operators.

CHAPTER EIGHT

Decoder installation

For many modern models, installing a decoder is as easy as removing a model's circuit board and plugging the new decoder into its socket. *Jeff Wilson*

Most new locomotives have some provision for Digital Command Control. This usually means they have a socket for a decoder and (hopefully) room for one. A growing number of new locomotives come with factory-installed decoders and include sound. These features are great when buying a new locomotive, but most of us have a collection of older locomotives that need conversion to DCC.

1 This steam locomotive tender (from a Bachmann HO scale 2-6-6-2) has a circuit board with an 8-pin socket. The plug for DC operation was removed, and the decoder can simply be plugged in. Note the "8" on the board indicating pin 8. A triangle is sometimes used to mark pin 1.

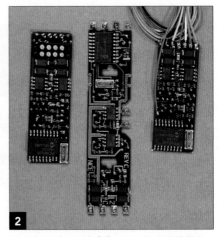

2 The decoder at left has an 8-pin NMRA connector. The middle decoder is a plug-and-play replacement board, and the decoder at right is a hard-wire decoder for non-DCC-ready models.

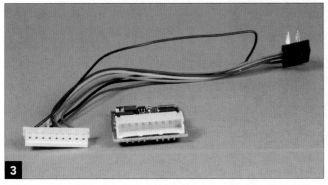

3 The compact JST connector, which has become very popular, uses nine in-line pins. The photo shows a cable that allows a 9-pin JST decoder to be plugged into an 8-pin socket.

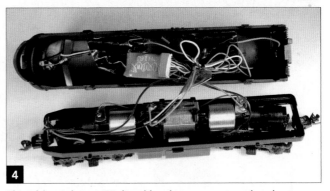

4 This older Athearn F7 diesel has been re-motored and converted to DCC with a Digitrax decoder. All decoder wiring connections are soldered.

Decoder trends

Newer decoders have more functions. Ditch lights, strobe lights, and interior cab lights are now all possible and can be controlled with the expanded number of function keys. Sound and motor control have also been improved. One great improvement has been the "super capacitor," which prevents locomotives from stalling due to dirty track and signal interruptions.

Atlas, Athearn, Bachmann, Broadway Limited Imports, Proto 2000 by Walthers, and others sell locomotives either with or without decoders installed. Many of these models are DC and DCC compatible with a full range of sound effects.

If you're buying a new locomotive without a decoder already installed, look for one marked "DCC Ready." Most models labeled as such have an 8-pin socket or the newer 9-pin JST socket with a small circuit board that can be unplugged so a compatible decoder can simply be plugged into the connector, **1**. For some models, it takes longer to figure out how to remove the body shell than it does to install a new decoder.

Some models have a standard size circuit board designed to be simply replaced by a standard DCC circuit board decoder, **2**.

The compact JST 9-pin connector, **3**, has become a standard connector in both locomotives and decoders. Digitrax makes a 3" wiring harness with an 8-pin connector on one end and the JST 9-pin socket on the other end (DHWHP). This lets you plug a JST decoder into a DCC-ready 8-pin model.

With the improved sound and

added lighting features of newer decoders, many modelers are now replacing older decoders. Adding back-electromotive-force control (back-EMF) for better motor control and improved sound is another reason for replacing older decoders.

Installing or replacing a hard-wired decoder—one that's soldered in place—can be time-consuming, **4**, but the process isn't complicated if you take it one wire at a time to transfer it to the new decoder.

Room for a decoder is scarce in many models, especially HO switchers and N scale locomotives, **5**. Because of this, many N scale decoders are custom-made to fit in a specific model. Companies like Aztec and Southern Digital offer milled frames for N scale locomotives, **6**. These frames allow room for non-custom decoders.

5 Some N scale decoders are designed to fit a specific series of locomotives. These are usually designed as replacements for the models' original circuit boards.

6 Aztec will mill your N scale locomotive frame to make room for a decoder. Shown is the frame for an N scale Atlas GP9.

Selecting a decoder

Begin by determining the current draw of the locomotive motor. Most decoders are rated for the stall current—the current draw at 12 volts with the motor stalled (not turning).

Some decoders are labeled for their intended scale, but the motor current —not the scale—is what's important. HO decoders work well in larger locomotives as long as their current rating is not exceeded, **7**. The most common ratings are 0.5 to 2 amps, but some decoders intended for large scale models are rated up to 10 amps.

Decoders also include function outputs for front and rear headlights, and newer decoders include additional function outputs. These can be programmed for effects such as Mars lights, ditch lights, strobe lights, firebox flicker, or various sounds. Function outputs have a maximum current rating that should not be exceeded. The function outputs on smaller decoders are rated at 100 milliamps (up to 1 amp on some larger decoders). See Chapter 9 for information on using lamps and light-emitting diodes (LEDs) with these outputs.

Sound is another factor to consider. Most sound decoders have low current ratings for use in smaller scales. For high-current motors, you can use a sound-only decoder along with a high-current decoder to match the motor.

If the locomotive has a coreless motor (found in some brass imports), be sure to use a decoder with a high-frequency motor drive. Most new decoders have this feature.

7 Shay No. 7 (top) has a sound decoder with a small speaker mounted at the bottom of the boiler. The On3 Climax (no. 8, bottom photo) uses an N scale decoder that fits under the oil tank. The model has a low enough current rating that the N scale decoder works and was easier to fit in the locomotive. Rio Grande no. 476 is equipped with an HO sound decoder.

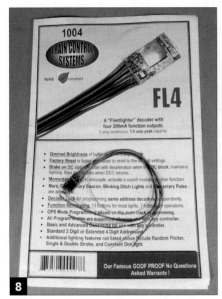

8

The Train Control Systems (TCS) Fleetlighter FL4 is a four-function decoder without motor control. It can be programmed with an address so you can control additional lighting functions on a locomotive or control lighting in a passenger car or caboose. The FL2 is a two-function version of this decoder.

Sometimes you need to add lights or another device but your decoder has run out of function outputs. The answer is a function-only decoder like the TCS FL4 with four outputs or the FL2 with two outputs, **8**.

DCC connections

The National Model Railroad Association (NMRA) has a standard color code for decoder wires, **9**. Connectors are covered by RP-9.1.1. The 8-pin dual-inline (two side-by-side rows of four pins) version, often generically referred to as the "NMRA plug," is the most popular. Of the eight pins, two go to the rails, two to the motor, and two to the lights, **10**. One is a common, and the last one a spare. When adding extra functions eight pins aren't enough. This is one reason the JST 9-pin connector has increased in popularity.

Some newer decoders with additional functions and 8-pin connectors have pads on their printed-circuit (PC) boards to solder the wires for extra functions and speakers. On the doodlebug shown in **11**, I soldered the wire from the interior passenger-compartment light to one of the extra function

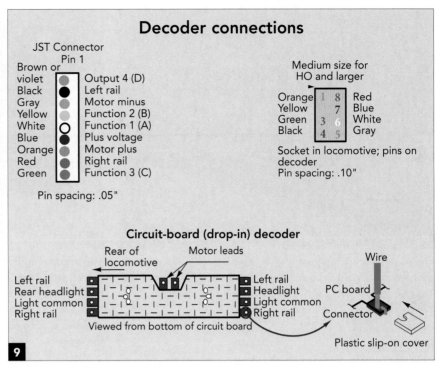

9

DCC decoders have color-coded wires and connectors. The colors follow standards established by the NMRA

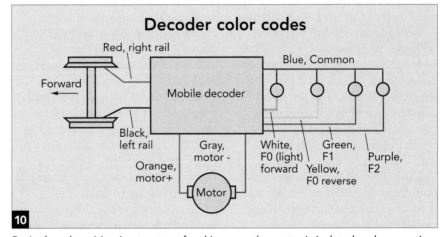

10

Basic decoder wiring is a matter of making sure the motor is isolated and connecting the rail, motor, and function outputs (headlights and other lights) properly.

outputs on the decoder board.

Drop-in circuit-board decoders are also popular, especially in N scale. Most locomotive models today carry wiring in circuit boards atop their chassis, so PC-board decoders (usually designed for a specific model) are simply swapped with the original circuit board, **12**.

Connections to PC-board decoders are often made by slipping a wire through a hole in a connector tab on the board, then sliding a plastic cover over the tab to hold the wire in place. Most models come with the covers

in place, allowing the wires to be transferred to the new decoder without having to unsolder connections. The connections on the decoder board are tinned so they can be soldered, which is the most reliable way to connect wires.

You can minimize errors when installing a PC-board decoder by moving one wire at a time from the old PC board to the new decoder.

Always test a locomotive on the programming track after installing or modifying a decoder, even after you've re-attached the shell to the chassis (the

11 The passenger compartment lights in each doodlebug were connected using an extra function (F3) on the decoder board. The two are consisted with one unit running backward so they can be run without turning them around.

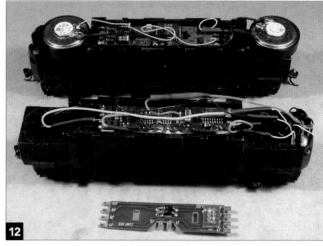

12 The decoder in the front locomotive (an HO Stewart F7A) controls the lights and motor. The B unit in the background has a sound decoder driving two speakers and the motor. The speakers are mounted in small enclosures and are facing downward. One of the models' original circuit boards is in the foreground.

pressure from the shell can easily drive two wires together, causing a short circuit). A short on the main line can mean a very short life for your decoder.

Before you modify a locomotive, determine whether there is a decoder designed to fit it. Some are designed as drop-in replacements for the existing circuit board. There are even sound decoders with speakers designed to fit into specific locomotive models.

It's almost impossible to keep up with all of the different decoders available, with installation information for different locomotives. Photos and decoder installation information can be found on many of the decoder manufacturers' Websites. A list of these manufacturers can be found in the appendix on page 86.

Hard-wiring decoders

The best way to connect wires without a connector is to solder them. It's important to insulate joints to prevent short circuits with other connections and parts of the frame or body. This is especially critical with metal locomotives and tenders. When you solder a connection, let the wire melt the solder, not the iron. A little solder on the clean tip of the iron will help transfer heat to the wire connection.

Heat-shrink tubing is the best choice to insulate connections.

Remember to slide a piece of tubing over the wire before you connect and solder the wires together. Liquid insulating fluid, such as Star Brite, can also be used. Black electrical tape doesn't work well, as it's difficult to apply in small areas and can come undone.

It's important to check the motor to be sure that it isn't connected to the frame. If you're unsure, check it with a continuity tester or an ohmmeter. Older Athearn models, for example, have the lower motor connection made directly to the metal frame.

To isolate the motor, **13**, remove the motor and bend flat the lower tangs that connect with the frame. You can also try moving the bottom strap to the top and the top to the bottom. Be careful when removing these straps as the springs under the straps hold the motor brushes in place. Put electrical tape or plastic over the frame to insulate it from the motor when it's replaced. Solder a wire to the lower motor strap while it is off the motor.

Lamps and LEDs

Check the locomotive's existing lamps to make sure they're compatible with the new decoder. Some manufacturers use 1.5-volt bulbs on the circuit boards, but these must have proper voltage— dropping resistors must be added or the

lamps replaced with 12-volt versions when installing a decoder. This is usually listed in the locomotive manual, but it can be easy to overlook. The best choice is to use LEDs instead of bulbs. (See chapter 9 for more on lighting.)

Pre-installation inspections

The first step before installing a decoder is to inspect the components. The locomotive should be run on DC to verify that it's operating correctly. If not, now is the time to fix it.

It's also a good idea to check the decoder, speaker, super capacitor module, and any other items that you'll be installing. Decoder testers are available from Ulrich (the former Loy's Toys tester), **14**, NCE, and ESU. These devices allow you to temporarily wire a decoder and test it. You can also set the address and make sure the functions work properly.

The NCE Decoder Tester (model DKT), **15**, has eight LEDs and a lamp. These show the status of some of the decoder's function outputs. The small lamp is used in place of a motor to act as a load. The load is needed when using the program track for feedback.

The NCE tester comes with two cables that connect to a decoder and both 8- and 9-pin plugs on the board. I find it convenient to mount the NCE tester on piece of plastic. I added a spare motor and speaker in an enclosure to use as a test load. You can add connectors to the ends of the one cable to attach the tester to decoders without the standard NMRA connectors. I prefer the hook-type instead of the alligator-type clips.

The ESU decoder tester, called the Proti-Tester (no. 51900), has LEDs, a motor, and speaker.

To test a decoder, it must have a motor or speaker load. The decoder responds to the read-back check by briefly turning the motor on which changes the current flow through the decoder. Without a load, there's no change in current flow, and the test fails even with a good decoder.

Once you've tested and installed a decoder, check it out on the programming track before placing it back into service. This alerts you to any short circuits that may have occurred during installation. Even if you've just pulled off the body shell and put it back on, check for shorts to be safe.

A "Can't Read CV" error message can be caused when the decoder draws too much current for the limited power

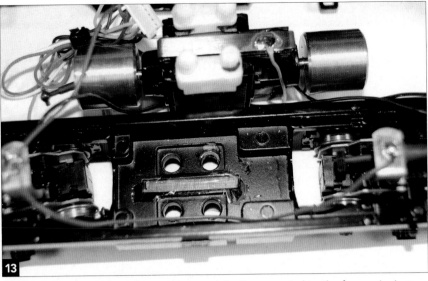

13

The motor on this older Athearn F7 was originally connected to the frame. A piece of Kapton tape over the original mounting area in the frame will insulate the motor from the frame. Make sure the prongs on the motor strap are flattened so it doesn't ground to the frame to the motor.

on the programming track. This can happen with some new sound decoders, and it can also happen with dual decoders in the same locomotive.

Super capacitor modules may also affect the read-back function. It's advisable to program the decoder before connecting the module.

To fix this, some firms make an adapter for their decoders. DCC Specialties' Power Pax and the SoundTraxx PTB-100boosters, **16**, take the program track data and boost it. The boosters use power from either a plug-in wall adapter or the power supplied to the command station, **17**.

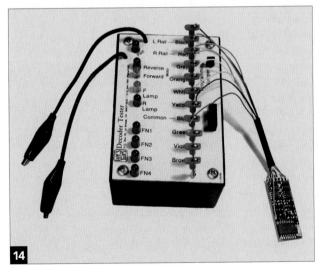

14

The Ulrich Decoder Tester DT-01 (formerly produced by Loy's Toys) lets you check a decoder before installation. It can also be used to program the decoder and check its address and functions. The tester uses light-emitting diodes, so if you're installing a decoder in a locomotive using lamps, there may be a difference in light response. The tester has spring clamps to connect the wires for the decoder to an 8-wire connector; an adapter cable is available for the 9-pin JST connector. The LEDs show the status of the decoder.

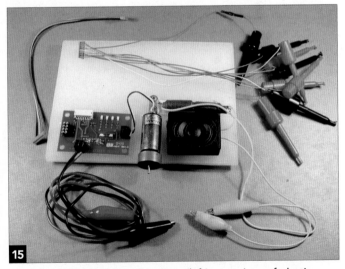

15

I mounted the NCE decoder tester (left) on a piece of plastic along with a speaker and motor. This allows testing both sound and motor operation. The tester has sockets for both 8- and 9-pin standard connectors. The added extra clips allow the tester to be connected to almost any decoder without a standard socket.

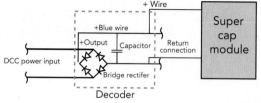

Adding a super capacitor module

This is how a super capacitor is connected to a decoder.

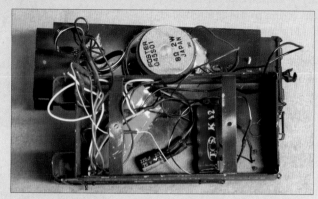

There is plenty of room to add the TCS KA (Keep-Alive) super capacitor module in this On3 tender.

Super capacitors, used to keep locomotives running over dirty track and keep passenger car lighting from flickering, have the highest available capacitance values per unit volume and the greatest energy density of all capacitors. Their capacity is so high they are measured in farads, not microfarads, with a capacitance value up to 10,000 times that of electrolytic capacitors. They bridge the gap between capacitors and rechargeable batteries.

However, super capacitors have a limitation: The maximum rated voltage of newer super capacitors is only 3-5 volts.

To get the voltage needed for DCC, capacitors have to be wired in series. This is like wiring batteries in series to get a higher voltage. With the 3-volt rating, about five capacitors in series are needed to work at DCC voltages.

When power is first applied, the capacitors need to be charged. To prevent overloading the system, charging is done slowly through a resistor. Wait a short time before running a locomotive so the capacitors can get some charge.

When the input voltage drops due to a bad connection, power is supplied to the decoder through a diode that bypasses the resistor. This is like an automobile battery and alternator. When the car is running, the battery charges. When stopped, the battery supplies the power. Even at slow speeds, locomotives with a super capacitor module will run through a dead turnout. A number of modelers have stated that a good running locomotive becomes an excellent runner with the module installed.

Installing super capacitor modules
Super capacitor modules need to be connected to the decoder leads supplying internal power to the decoder. Basically, the module needs to be connected to the output of the bridge rectifier in the decoder.

Normally the blue wire from the decoder is the positive lead from the bridge rectifier. You also need to connect the negative output (return or common connection) of the rectifier. There are two possible problems here. Not all of the positive (blue leads) are directly connected to the decoder bridge rectifier. Some are designed to supply a lower voltage to operate lamps and LEDs. Other decoders

use a black or black/white lead for the return (negative) connection to the bridge rectifier. It's beyond the scope of this book to cover the various decoder wiring possibilities. Here is one place where one of the Internet groups can help. Most likely someone else has run into the same wiring problem you have.

My best suggestion is to examine the decoder before you install the super capacitor module. This gives you a chance to determine the correct polarity on the decoder before you wire it. If you wire the module in reverse, you can destroy the super capacitor, which may void your warranty.

There have also been reports of problems when programming decoders with super cap modules attached.

You can connect super capacitor modules to a decoder with a two-wire miniature connector, such as Miniatronics 50-001 micro-mini connectors. If you're worried about accidentally reversing the connector, use a three-wire connector and wire the two outside wires to the common return and the power on the middle only—no matter which way you plug it in it will still work.—*Don Fiehmann*

Refer to the manufacturer's instructions for information on connecting and using a programming track booster.

Installing dual decoders
There are a number of reasons to install two decoders and use the same address for both decoders. An example

is installing a sound-only decoder in a locomotive also equipped with a motor/light decoder. You can also use a second decoder to add additional lighting effects and control, **8**.

As mentioned in Chapter 5, you can use two decoders with the same address in locomotives that are always paired, such as an A-B set of F units.

When installing a second decoder in a single locomotive, you can hardwire (solder) the sound and motor decoders together or use a two-pin connector, **18**. Connectors can be quite handy for steam locomotives, too, as a two- or three-pin connector can be used between the locomotive and tender, **19**.

16

Two programming track boosters are the DCC Specialties Power Pax (left) and SoundTraxx PTB-100.

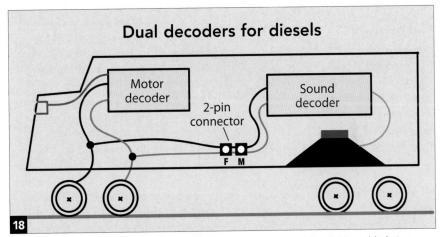

17

The booster is wired between the programming track output of the command station and the program track.

Lock feature on dual decoders

Digitrax offers a lock feature that allows you to individually write to just one decoder in a dual-decoder installation. The lock feature is in the NMRA DCC specifications and can be found in a growing number of decoders, including SoundTraxx Tsunami and newer Digitrax decoders.

The lock feature uses CVs 15 and 16. To use it, set CV16 to a different control value in each decoder. Then write a matching value to CV15 when you program that decoder. The other decoder's CVs will not match, so only the matching decoder will be programmed. If CVs 15 and 16 don't match, the decoder is locked and you can't program that decoder.

This is also something to consider if you have problems programming a decoder. Check to make sure

that CVs 15 and 16 haven't been accidentally changed. They must match to be able to program the decoder.

A tip I found on the Internet works almost as well on decoders without the

lock feature. Use a two-digit address for both decoders: for example, "01" for the motor decoder and "02" for the second (sound) decoder. When you connect the two decoders, they can

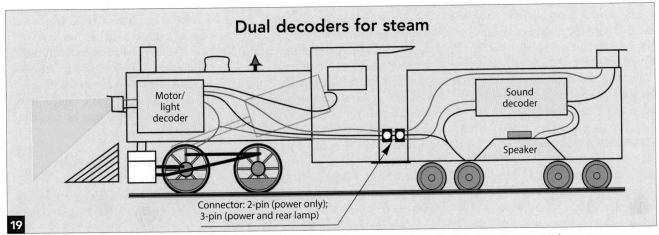

18

A second decoder in a diesel locomotive can control sound or additional lighting effects such as ditch lights or rooftop strobes. Adding a connector between the two to makes it easier to program and troubleshoot.

19

Here's one way to wire a sound-only decoder in a tender with a motor decoder in the boiler. (See Chapter 10 for more information on wiring sound decoders.)

Decoder installation tools

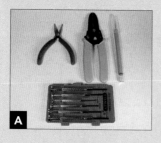

To install anything other than a plug-in decoder, you'll need a few tools and supplies for installing decoders and upgrading lighting. You probably already have many of these items from general modeling.

In buying tools, I follow the philosophy that you will soon forget the price of a high-quality tool, but you'll cuss a cheap tool every time you use it!

Tools and materials (A, B)
- Hobby knife
- Motor tool
- Small diagonal wire cutter and wire stripper for small wire
- Small needle-nose pliers
- Small screwdriver set
- Double-sided foam tape (to attach the decoder)
- Thin heat-resistant tape (such as

Kapton)
- Assorted small sizes of heat-shrink tubing
- RTV adhesive (for mounting speakers)
- Fine rosin-core solder
- Fine wire (28 or 30 gauge)

Soldering wires (C)
Use a small pencil-style soldering iron (35 watts or less). Make sure you slide the heat-shrink tubing over the wire before you solder it. Use a wire stripper designed for small wire, such as the Micro-Mark no. 14221. Wrap the two wires together, then heat the wire with the soldering iron. The tip of the iron should be clean and have some solder on it to help transfer heat from the iron to the wire. It's important that you get the wire hot enough to melt the solder, then touch the solder to the wire, not the iron.

A heat gun can be hard to handle when sealing heat-shrink tubing on small wire. There's also the danger of accidentally heating something that you didn't want heated. Instead, I use a small candle. Hold the lit candle below the heat-shrink tubing, but don't let the flame touch the tubing. Miniatronics sells a package of mixed small sizes of shrink tubing.

Multimeter (D)
Some multi-meters have a continuity check feature. This can be very useful when determining whether a motor is connected to the frame of an engine. I find the inexpensive RadioShack meter shown (no. 22-802) to be very useful. This meter also has a continuity check plus a diode check function.

---

be addressed to the same four-digit address.

When set for a four-digit address, CV29 has bit 5 on. With ops mode programming, you can change CV29 to a value of "2," and the decoders will both be in two-digit mode. Now you can work with either decoder separately using its two-digit address. When finished, use the ops mode to change CV29 back to four-digit addressing. This takes two steps. You need to write back CV29 to address "01," and then address "02" separately.

Accessory decoders

Accessory decoders to control switch machines are normally mounted under a layout where their size isn't important. The key consideration in selecting an accessory decoder is the type of switch machine or motor that you are using—not the scale, **20, 21**.

There are two basic types of switch machines: the coil or solenoid, which snaps the points into place; and the slow-motion stall-motor type. Both of these can be divided into two more categories, high-current and low-current.

Some accessory decoders are designed to drive a particular type of switch machine, and others are programmable and can drive many types of machines, **22** and **23**. Most decoders use capacitor discharge for twin coil switch machines. When programmed to operate multiple machines, most decoders only have enough power to line one switch at a time. The decoder lines a turnout, delays to recharge the capacitor, then lines the next turnout.

Power for accessory decoders and switch machines can come from the DCC signal/power bus that feeds the

rails or from a separate power source. With some accessory decoders, the choice of the power source is optional. Check the manual for each decoder (usually available on the manufacturer's Website).

Most accessory decoders can be controlled by either a DCC command or push-button switches. Some manufacturers' basic cabs and throttles will operate locomotives, but can't issue accessory decoder commands. If your operators have only basic cabs, a push-button control panel may be needed for turnout operation.

Programming accessory decoders

Most accessory decoders use a jumper or wire connection for programming (not the programming track). Set the programming mode on the decoder, turn on the DCC power, and then

20 The Digitrax DS64 accessory decoder can control four switch machines.

21 The Wabbit dual-accessory decoder can operate two Tortoise (Circuitron) stall-motor switch machines.

22 Stationary decoder and switch machine compatibility

Decoder Switch Type	Digitrax			Lenz		DCC Specialties		NCE			Team Digital	CVP	
	DS44	DS52	DS64	LS 100	LS 150	Hare	Wabbit	Switch-it	Snap-it	Switch-Kat	SMD2 SMD8	AD4MC	AD4H
Switch motor Type A1	Yes	Yes	Yes	OK[1]	Poor[2]	Tortoise Only	Tortoise Only	Yes	No	No	Poor	Yes	No
Switch motor Type A2	No	Yes	Yes	No	Yes	No	No	No	No	No	No	?	No
Twin-coil Type B1	No	Yes	Yes	Yes	Yes	No	No	No	Yes	No	Yes	No	Yes
Twin-coil Type B2	No	Yes	No	Yes	No	No	No	No	Yes[3]	No	Yes	No	Yes
Kato or LGB	No	Yes	Yes	No	Yes	No	No	No	No	Yes	No	Yes	No
Number of outputs	4	4	4	4	6	1	2	2	1	1	2/8	4/8	4

[1]LA 010 Required for this output.   [2]Output not continuous.   [3]May need to add a capacitor for high-current machines.

Accessory decoders with multiple outputs can control several switch machines at once. This is especially handy in staging and other yards, where a single command can align all the turnouts for a yard track. Many multiple-output accessory decoders order the outputs so only one turnout is thrown at a time. This is more typical of capacitor-discharge decoders where the timing allows the capacitor to recharge. The Hare and its bigger brother, the Wabbit, are intelligent accessory decoders that can be wired to automatically throw a turnout if a train approaches and the turnout is set the wrong way (eliminating a possible short circuit). The Hare also lets you feed back the switch position to the command station. You can also use these decoders to program routes, whereby the decoder will tell other Hares and Wabbits which turnout to set. This is helpful if your DCC system doesn't offer macro or route-control features.

issue the accessory address commands. With a Digitrax system, turn on the system before connecting the decoder to be programmed. Some Digitrax systems send out a few packets when first turned on, which can cause incorrect programming.

Turn the power off, put the accessory decoder back into run mode, and the accessory decoder will respond to the programmed address.

23 Switch machine brands

Motor-driven		Twin-coil	
Stall (Type A1)	Power cut-off (Type A2)	Low- to medium-current (Type B1)	High-current (Type B2)
Micro-Mark, Tortoise, and SwitchMaster	PFM/Fulgerex and Scale Shops[1]	Atlas and Peco	Rix, NJI, and Tenshodo

[1]May need series lamp or resistor to reduce voltage.

CHAPTER NINE

Using LEDs and bulbs with DCC

Headlights, ditch lights (on the BNSF locomotive at left) and rooftop beacons or strobes (right) are just a few of the lighting effects available with DCC. *Bill Zuback*

Lighting has always been important part of the appearance of an operating locomotive. With Digital Command Control (DCC), constant lighting with controllable front and rear headlights is standard. Digital Command Control makes many other lighting effects easy to add and remotely control, including simulated Mars (rotating) lights, strobe and warning beacons, ditch lights, firebox flicker, and dimmable headlights. The new surface-mount device (SMD) light-emitting diodes make it possible to put light in extremely small places.

The locomotive headlight on the left is an incandescent bulb, the one in the middle is an older bluish-tint white LED, and the model at right has a Yeloglo LED designed to emit a color more like an bulb.

Lamps vs. LEDs

Light-emitting diodes (LEDs) have been replacing lamps (bulbs) in models for some time, and many new locomotive models come with LEDs. There are good reasons for this. Incandescent lamps and LEDs both produce light, but they have significantly different electrical characteristics. Also, although LEDs were once expensive, they're now as cheap or cheaper than lamps. Here are some key differences:

First, LEDs are about 80 percent more efficient than lamps. Lamps require a short warmup time, and electrical resistance changes significantly as the lamp heats up. A cold lamp has about a tenth of the resistance of an operating lamp. Miniature lamps are available in a range of voltages from 1.5 to 16 volts, with current ratings of 15 to 100 milliamps. Lamps act like a resistor, and current can flow both ways through them.

An LED comes on instantly when power is applied, and its resistance remains constant. Light-emitting diodes normally operate on just a few volts and less than 20 milliamps. Since LEDs are diodes, current flows in only one direction, so LEDs must be wired with the correct polarity.

Low-voltage lamps and LEDs require a series resistor to match their low operating voltage to the output voltage of a decoder. The value of the series resistor used with a lamp is

critical; not so with LEDs. A 1K-ohm (1,000-ohm) to 3K-ohm (3,000-ohm) resistor in series works fine most of the time. Newer LEDs are more efficient and may need a higher resistor value if the LED is too bright.

LEDs begin producing light at a very low current. This light remains fairly constant, not growing much brighter from about 5 milliamps to the maximum of 20 milliamps.

Lamps emit light in all directions; an LED's light is directional, like a flashlight.

Heat can be a problem with lamps. One modeler told me his experience of using two lamps for the front headlight of a diesel. After leaving the lights on for some time, the lamps melted part of the plastic shell.

Real locomotive headlights are a slightly yellowish white. Newer LEDs, such as Yeloglo, produce a yellowish color that closely resembles that of an incandescent lamp, **1**. Older "white" LEDs have a cool, bluish appearance similar to that of a fluorescent light; they can be tinted with yellow transparent paint or a felt-tip pen to improve the color.

Lamps and LEDs are both available in small sizes, **2**. Common sizes are 1.5mm, 3mm, and 5mm. These are mounted on PC boards in some locomotives.

Surface-mount-device (SMD) LEDs are handy when light is needed

in small places, **3**. They'll easily fit into a Z scale headlight or HO marker lantern, **4**. There are many small sizes and colors available. A good source of SMD LEDs, including SMD resistors and thin wire, is Ngineering (www.ngineering.com). Like other LEDs, SMD's require a dropping resistor in series to control the current.

Lamps have a life expectancy rated in hours, while the life of an LED is rated in years. White LEDs cost about $1 each. A properly installed LED will outlast the locomotive, and the LED cost is certainly cheaper than your time to replace a burned-out bulb.

For headlights or strobes, either lamps or LEDs can be used. However, for special effects like headlight dimming and Mars lights, there's a difference in response time and current sensitivity. These effects are controlled by pulse-width modulation (PWM), the same method the decoder uses to control motor speed.

Some decoders use a bit in the lighting-control CV to change the characteristic of the function output to better match an LED for special effects. Before using an LED for special lighting, check to see whether your decoder supports LEDs.

To determine the PWM difference between an LED and a lamp, I connected an oscilloscope to a decoder's lighting function output. To dim a lamp, the function output was on 37

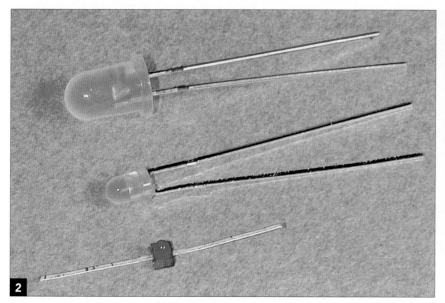

Three common LED sizes are (from top) 5mm, 3mm, and 1.5mm. LEDs come in many colors, including white.

These two surface-mount device (SMD) LEDs are soldered to magnet wire. The smaller is a 401 and the other a 603. Ngineering is a good source for the SMD and accessories. *Howard McKinney*

This On3 caboose uses a function-only decoder to control the lights. The marker lights use SMD LEDs. *Howard McKinney*

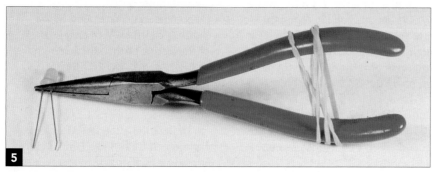

Pliers clamped to the leads just below the LED serve as a heat sink to protect the LED during soldering.

percent of the time. However, to make an LED appear to dim, the output was on only 6 percent of the time.

Decoder manuals

Check the decoder's manual when wiring lamps and LEDs. Some decoders use built-in resistors or voltage regulators to reduce the output voltage/power to match low-voltage lamps and LEDs.

Check existing bulbs when installing a decoder in a DCC-ready locomotive. Many models use diodes to reduce the voltage to the lamps, and connecting the existing lamps to a decoder may burn out the bulbs. Check the locomotive's instruction sheet to determine if the lamps need to be replaced.

If you're unsure of a lamp's voltage, test it with a 1.5-volt battery. If it lights brightly, it's a 1.5-volt bulb. If it doesn't light, it's either a higher-rated bulb or burned out—test it using a higher voltage.

Wiring

Lights are normally wired from the blue (common) wire on the decoder to one of the function outputs. The blue wire is the positive (+) connection and the function outputs are the negative (-) connections. Lamps and LEDs can be connected to the same decoder; for

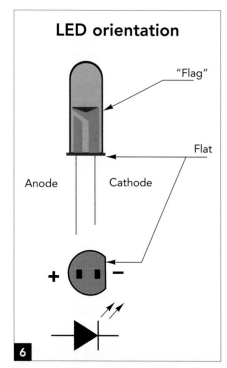

LED orientation

"Flag"

Flat

Anode   Cathode

+ ▪▪ −

6

Since an LED is a diode, it must be wired with the correct polarity to work.

7 Resistor values for bulbs

Bulb current (milliamps)	Track voltage (true RMS)								Resistor rating
	12.5	13	13.5	14	14.5	15	15.5	16	
15	680	680	720	750	820	820	910	910	¼ watt
30	330	360	360	390	390	430	430	470	½ watt
40	240	270	270	300	300	300	330	330	1 watt
50	200	200	220	220	240	240	270	270	1 watt
60	160	180	180	200	200	200	220	220	1 watt
80	120	130	130	150	150	160	160	160	2 watt

It's important to use the proper resistor when using bulbs for lighting. This chart, with resistor values listed in ohms, is courtesy of NCE. The resistor value for LEDs is not as critical as with lamps.

example, a lamp for the headlight and an LED for a rooftop beacon.

When soldering LED leads, be careful not to excessively heat the LED itself. Needlenose pliers can be used between the soldering iron and LED as a heat sink, 5.

Lamps aren't polarity sensitive, but LEDs require a resistor. The cathode of the LED must be connected to the function output. The cathode is the lead next to the flat side of the LED, 6.

Insulate all connections to lamps, LEDs, and resistors to prevent short circuits with other connections and the locomotive itself. Use either paint-on insulation or heat-shrink tubing. Be sure to insulate the wires to lamps and LEDs before putting the body shell back on. I blew out the function outputs of two decoders before I discovered that the strobe LED leads were shorting each time the shell was replaced. A piece of tape over the bare LED leads cured this. Kapton tape (available from Digi-Key and Tony's Train Exchange) works well for this.

When installing LEDs, check the decoder manual for resistors, the amount of power and voltage on the blue lead, and factory-installed dropping resistors in the function

output.

Also check if the decoder provides 5 volts for lamps and LEDs. Light-emitting diodes require series resistance to reduce the current. The voltage drop across an LED varies with the color. For red or green LEDs it is usually about 2 volts, white LEDs around 3 volts.

Resistor values for lamps

You'll need a resistor in series with 12- to 14-volt lamps to protect the decoder from high start-up current. Decoder manuals recommend a 22- to 33-ohm resistor for lamps rated at more than 40 milliamps. A series resistor will also increase the life of the lamp.

If you have a 1.5-volt lamp and require a series resistor, check the chart, 7, to determine the proper value. Normal track voltage is 13 to 14 volts, and there is some voltage loss before the power reaches the output. If you're using multiple lamps on the same function output, each lamp requires its own resistor, 8. If a single resistor feeds more than one lamp, and one lamp burns out, the full current will go to the other lamp, resulting in two burned out lamps.

Diode regulator

You can also use a diode regulator to control lamp voltage, 9. This circuit uses two 1N4001 silicon diodes. The advantage is that more than one lamp can be connected to the same circuit.

With this circuit, lamp brightness remains constant when track voltage varies. It requires a few more parts

but is trouble-free and well worth the effort. The series resistor should supply adequate current for the lamps used. Any excess current is bypassed through the diodes. Each diode has a .7-volt drop, for a combined drop of 1.4 volts. Lamps can be wired in parallel with this circuit.

Resistor value for LEDs

For LEDs the solution is simple: use a 1K- to 3K-ohm ¼-watt resistor in series with the LED. I've wired as many as three LEDs (one white and two red) in series with a 1K-ohm resistor with good results. For more than 15 volts, use a ½-watt 1K-ohm resistor or a ¼-watt 1.5K-ohm resistor.

If space is tight, ⅛-watt resistors are available. However, at ⅛ watt, a 1K-ohm resistor in series with an LED will be close to its maximum power rating. The resistor may get hot, which can damage a plastic shell. A higher value such as a 1.5K- to 3K-ohm ⅛-watt resistor will run cooler but will give just a slight reduction in light output. This may not be a problem because newer LEDs are more efficient. Use a resistor value that gives the light output that you need—just don't exceed the LED or decoder rating.

Layout power indicator

There are many uses for LEDs as indicators. One is to use a bicolor LED to show power on track, 10. You'll need a bi-color LED and a 1K-ohm, ½-watt resistor. The LED can be mounted on a control panel or on the fascia. Normally it should be yellow—off

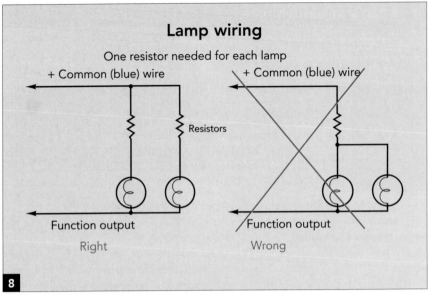

Lamp wiring

One resistor needed for each lamp

+ Common (blue) wire

Resistors

Function output

Right

+ Common (blue) wire

Function output

Wrong

8

When wiring 1.5-volt lamps, each bulb requires its own resistor. Light-emitting diodes can be wired in series with a limiting resistor.

means there's no power, and red or green may indicate a problem with the booster. If your system has the option of running a locomotive without a decoder, a color change may just show the biased DCC signal (stretched zero) used to run non-decoder locomotives.

Programming, key mapping

Decoder manuals list the CV values for different lighting effects. These values control the type of lighting and the conditions under which they operate —for example, dimming a headlight in the reverse direction. These special lighting effects can be tested on the layout using ops mode (on-the-fly) programming, explained in Chapter 5.

I have an On3 railbus with all the bells, whistles, and lights of the proto-

New use for an old decoder

A

B

C

D

The lights at this factory are controlled with a mobile decoder. The lights can be all off (A), all on (B), streetlights only on (C), or warehouse and streetlights on (D).

Most of us eventually end up with old, unused mobile decoders on hand. There's no reason why these can't be used for stationary applications, such as building lighting.

The building shown above has lights in the office area, separate lights in the warehouse, and streetlights along the edge of the driveway. I used a decoder's function output for the LED streetlights

and the motor output for the lamps in the warehouse and office.

The office lights are wired through a diode, but the other lights aren't. By switching the decoder from forward to reverse, the lights in the office turn off; the warehouse and streetlights stay on. A trick is to set speed step one to full power and momentum to zero. This allows the lights to come on to full

brightness without going through all the speed steps.

Using old mobile decoders for stationary applications has many possibilities beyond lighting, including powering a windmill or controlling the speed of an oil pumping station. Power for the decoder should be wired before any rail detectors, or it may cause erratic signal operation.
—*Don Fiehmann*

type, **11**. The four function outputs of the SoundTraxx decoder are wired for forward headlight, backup light, rooftop strobe, and an exhaust flicker. I often forgot which function keys turned on the different lights. Using key mapping, I set it up so F0 would activate all four lights. (The headlight and backup lights go on only when the correct direction is set.) I connected the headlight and two red LEDs (rear markers) in series with a 1K-ohm resistor; these all are on when the railbus moves forward.

On an N scale diesel with a Digitrax decoder, I set the key mapping so F3 turns on both the headlight and reverse lights. I can turn both lights on and off to see if I have control of the locomotive. The lights work normally when F3 is off.

Passenger car lighting

I visited a layout with a string of new passenger cars on a siding—and their interior lights were blinking on and off. The circuit breaker for that section of track couldn't handle the starting current for the lamps in that many cars. When a few cars were removed, the lights were OK, even after the other cars were replaced. This is the same overload startup problem that plagues some newer sound-equipped engines.

The best solution is to use LEDs instead of lamps. Miniatronics offers several kits, **12**. The LEDs use less than half the power of bulbs, have no high startup current, and have a super capacitor that provides flicker-free lighting. I tested a lamp against an LED light bar for passenger car operation. At 13 volts, the lamp used 120 milliamps and the LEDs only 45mA.

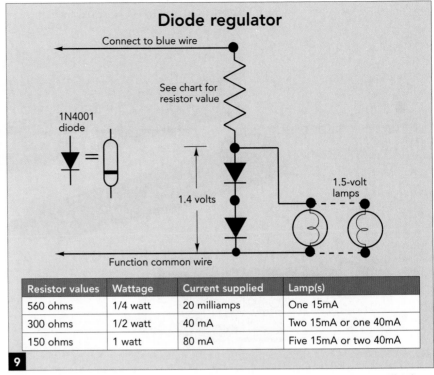

Diode regulator

Resistor values	Wattage	Current supplied	Lamp(s)
560 ohms	1/4 watt	20 milliamps	One 15mA
300 ohms	1/2 watt	40 mA	Two 15mA or one 40mA
150 ohms	1 watt	80 mA	Five 15mA or two 40mA

9 This circuit supplies a constant 1.4 volts that can be used for 1.5-volt lamps. This list of resistors is based on the maximum wattage of the resistors with a 14-volt input to the decoder.

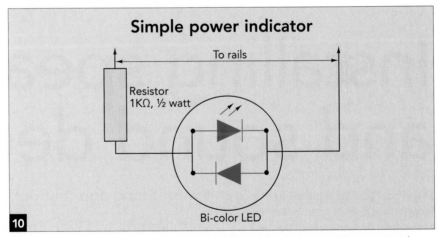

Simple power indicator

10 This circuit monitors the power on the rails. The LED can be located on a control panel or on the fascia near the track area.

11 This railbus has a headlight, rooftop strobe, two rear marker lights, and an exhaust flicker light. Remapping the function keys allows all of the lights to be turned on with one function key.

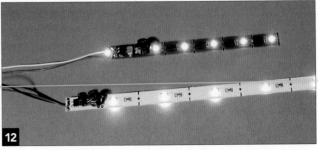

12 Miniatronics makes two LED light bars for car interiors: a short one for N scale passenger cars or HO cabooses and a longer one for HO passenger cars. The LEDs are powered from the rails and use a super capacitor for flicker-free lighting.

CHAPTER TEN

Installing speakers and sound decoders

Sound decoders are available to fit most locomotives, even N scale models such as this Kato F7 with an MRC 0001957 decoder. The circuit-board-style decoder has the speaker and a headlight LED built into the board. *David Popp*

It wasn't long ago that options for model railroad sound were limited. In 1980, Onboard offered a choice of steam or diesel sounds with a couple of whistle variations that were set with switches on the receiver in the locomotive. Dynatrol had steam exhaust and air pump sounds, and there were a few other proprietary systems. All of these early systems produced a limited number of sounds.

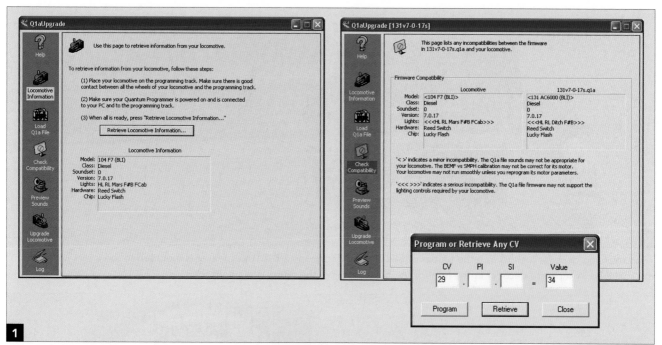

1 These screen shots from QSI's programming software show how it can read data from a locomotive (left). Once the data is read, you can select another sound file (right). The program will show potential compatibility problems (lighting on this example). A separate program supplied with the QSI programmer allows modifying configuration variables (lower right) and testing the sound file.

Then came Digital Command Control (DCC), and sound choices expanded with SoundTraxx's sound decoders. The number of manufacturers making sound decoders continues to grow, along with the variety and quality of locomotive sounds. Downloadable sound files allow modelers to not only choose steam, diesel, or electric locomotives, but in many cases select sounds to match a specific locomotive. Sounds like wheel squeal, air pumps, and dynamic braking are added to engine sounds. Sound quality has been improved by replacing 8-bit sound with 16-bit sound. Some of the sound decoders have provisions for using two speakers in stereo.

Manufacturers

SoundTraxx offers the Tsunami DSD line of basic decoders in HO and N scales and also makes a line of sound-only decoders. The Tsunami is SoundTraxx's premium line of 16-bit

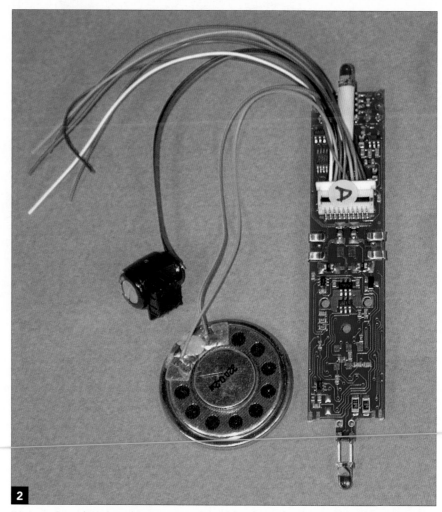

2 Digitrax SoundFX decoders use downloadable sounds. This decoder is designed to replace the circuit board on a Kato HO AC4400, SD38-2, or F40PH. Since the decoder can also be used with steam engines, it has a cam input for synchronization of steam chuffs.

This LokSound decoder just fits into the tender of this N scale Bachmann 2-8-2. The speaker is mounted in the insert just under the coal load. A separate decoder in the front of the boiler controls the motor and headlight.

In order to replace a sound file in a decoder, a programmer is used. From left to right are the Digitrax PR-2 (the PR-3 is now available), the QSI Solutions, and the LokSound Programmer. All three come with a CD that includes the necessary software. New sound files can be downloaded via the Internet. Since there is no standard for programmers, each programmer only works with its own line of decoders.

sound decoders, with many added detail effects like the sound of water filling the tender that ends with a squeaky hatch closing with a bang.

The Tsunami has a built-in sound equalizer so the output can adjust the sound to match the speaker. Each Tsunami decoder offers a choice of whistles that can be selected by the value in a configuration variable (CV). Chuff sounds are also adjustable so they're heavier when working and shortened when slowing down. The Tsunami also includes back-electromotive-force controls (back-EMF). The Tsunami is used in some ready-to-run locomotives. Protocraft has a modified 3.5 amp version of the Tsunami for larger scales.

QSI makes the Quantum Sound line of decoders that are in many ready-to-run locomotives. QSI also makes aftermarket decoders available for installation in non-sound-equipped locomotives. The newest Q3 versions of these decoders feature improved 16-bit sounds and back-EMF. The

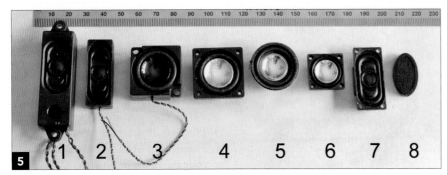

5 Small speakers are available in all shapes and sizes. *Adrian Pardon*

The easiest place to mount a speaker in a steam locomotive is the tender under the coal load.

decoder even has a stereo output to drive two speakers. The QSI decoders have downloadable sounds and a programmer that makes it easy to modify sounds and other features, **1**.

The new TCS (Train Control Systems) line of sound decoders is called WOWSound. The new decoder incorporates all of the latest technology, including a super-capacitor module and 16-bit sound. There is a demo on YouTube showing a locomotive running slowly through turnouts with dead frogs and over about a foot of track covered with a piece of cloth. The WOW series started with three steam sound versions. The decoders have an Audio Assist feature to help with ops-mode programming. The decoder will talk you through the setup of lights and sound. You can hear the sound and select it or try another using function keys.

Digitrax makes a line of sound decoders for general installation, some drop-in decoders for N and HO scale locomotives, and a sound-only decoder. The firm also offers a wide variety of SoundFX decoders, **2**, to fit many different locomotives. You'll need to have a Digitrax SFX decoder installed to take advantage of Digitrax's downloadable files. The decoder has an equalizer that allows you to adjust the sound to match the speaker. Digitrax also has a sound editor that lets you create a sound file from your own recordings.

LokSound sound decoders are imported from Germany and made by Electronic Solutions Ulm (ESU). These decoders can be programmed with sound files from a wide variety of European and North American locomotives. They feature back-

EMF and are equipped with 100-ohm speakers. The standard line is designed to fit mainly HO and larger locomotives.

LokSound also offers the LokSound Micro for N scale, **3**. This decoder comes with a 0.62"-diameter, 100-ohm speaker and is compatible with LokSound 3.5 sound files. ESU offers a programmer that connects to the serial port of a PC, either the RS232 or USB. The programmer, **4**, allows you to change the sound file in a decoder or install your own custom sounds. You can even change the characteristics of an existing sound file.

MRC makes the Brilliance line of steam and diesel sound decoders. Various whistles and horns are factory loaded and can be selected with CV settings. This series of decoders has limited back-EMF. The original release was intended for HO and larger models, and MRC has also come out with a smaller version for N scale.

Installing sound

Many locomotive makers have teamed up with sound decoder manufacturers to produce ready-to-run sound-

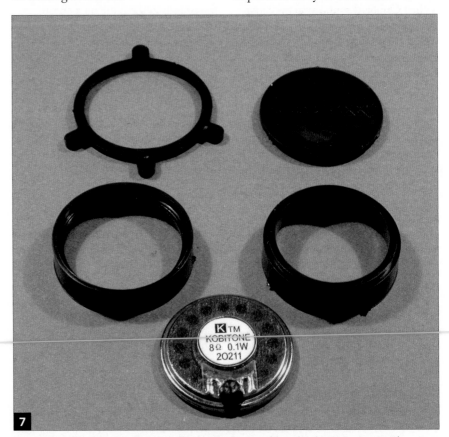

7 Tony's Train Exchange offers matching speakers and handy plastic snap-together speaker enclosures.

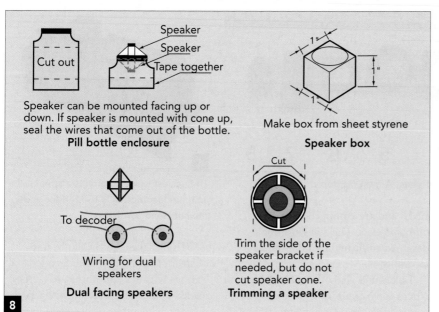

Pill bottle enclosure
Cut out
Speaker
Speaker
Tape together
Speaker can be mounted facing up or down. If speaker is mounted with cone up, seal the wires that come out of the bottle.

Speaker box
Make box from sheet styrene
1"
1"
1"

Dual facing speakers
To decoder
Wiring for dual speakers

Trimming a speaker
Cut
Trim the side of the speaker bracket if needed, but do not cut speaker cone.

8

Speaker enclosures can be made in several ways. Many ready-made speaker enclosures are available. Dual facing speakers act as their own baffles.

equipped engines. Others provide space in the locomotive frame for speakers. Some decoders are designed to operate on either DC or DCC (dual mode).

Programmable decoders

When Onboard sound systems came out, modelers were happy to have a choice of either steam or diesel sounds. However, these generic sounds just don't cut it anymore. Just as modelers now demand more detail in locomotive models, they also want accuracy in the sounds they produce. An EMD GP9 should have the sound of a 567 engine, not just a generic diesel.

A big problem for manufacturers and dealers is trying to stock all the variations of steam, diesel, and electric locomotive decoders. One solution is downloadable sound files, either on a CD or over the Internet.

The Digitrax and LokSound programmers both allow modelers to make their own sound files. If you can't locate the desired sound files, you can piece one together from different sound files or record your own. These options take some learning and time, but the potential is great.

I have a LokSound decoder and programmer, which runs on Windows on a PC. My decoder was programmed for an F7 diesel with a single-chime air horn, but I wanted to install it in

the tender of an Athearn 2-8-2 steam locomotive. Using the programmer, I selected a steam sound file, and then downloaded it to the decoder.

The LokSound programmer has limited power and will let you operate the sounds and engine on a short section of track with the PC.

Because technology is always advancing and new products are always arriving, manufacturers' Websites are the best sources for up-to-date information on sound systems. Many sites provide sound samples that you can download and play.

They talk back to you

A new feature that makes programming sound decoders easier is voice feedback. Both the QSI and TCS decoders have a verbal feedback feature to assist with programming. The verbal response feature is used as a feedback when programming on the main.

The "talk-back" feature should be turned off when using Java Model Railroad Interface (JMRI) due to timing problems. Profiles are available for most sound decoders, and new files are created as new decoders are released.

Sound synchronization

The classic way to synchronize steam engine exhaust chuffs with the rotation

of the drivers is with a cam or photo sensor on a driver axle, which can be difficult to install. Newer sound decoders allow the chuff rate to be controlled by the value in a CV to match the driver rotation. These are easy to set, although the sync accuracy may vary with speed. If accurate synchronization is important to you, choose a sound decoder with a cam input.

Real diesel engines have variable speeds, typically using eight speed notches. Auto notch or the number of speed steps per notch can be set by a value in a CV with some decoders.

Speaker types

Speakers come in many sizes. All are rated by their impedance in ohms. It's important to use a speaker with the proper impedance. Originally, sound decoders used 8-ohm impedance speakers. However, Digitrax now attaches 32-ohm speakers to its decoders, and the LokSound decoder comes with a .91"-diameter, 100-ohm speaker and an enclosure. SoundTraxx, QSI, TCS's WOWSound, and MRC all use 8-ohm speakers.

For best results, use only the speakers recommended by the manufacturer. Distortion or damage can occur if the wrong speaker type is used. Tony's Train Exchange has a line of high-bass speakers and enclosures in many sizes. Speakers are also available in variety of sizes and shapes to fit specific models, 5. TVW Miniatures offers round and rectangle-shaped cell phone speakers and laser-cut enclosures, which are ideal for models where space is at a premium.

Some sound decoders come with a small capacitor that must be wired in series with the speaker. Most of these capacitors are bipolar and can be installed without polarity concern. The capacitor leads should be protected from short circuits with heat-shrink tubing or paint-on insulation. Purple wire is used for speakers on most sound decoders.

Installing speakers

Sound decoders are about the same size as non-sound decoders—the difference is the speaker(s). To get

9

Oval speakers allow placing a larger speaker in a smaller body. Many sizes of speakers are available.

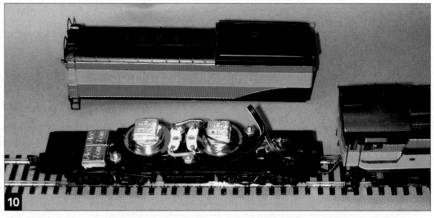

10

This HO brass steam locomotive has a Tsunami sound decoder installed in the boiler above the motor. To get the maximum amount of low frequency sounds for the whistle, two large oval speakers (wired in series) were installed facing down in the tender.

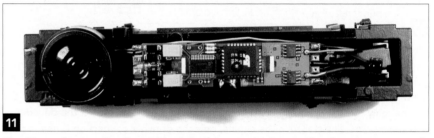

11

The 1" speaker just fits the width of the frame in this B unit. The decoder comes with plugs to connect the speaker wires, but I found it easier to solder them in place (as with the rest of the wires to the decoder).

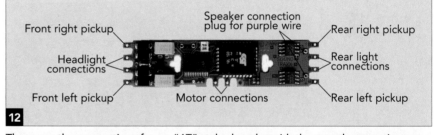

12

These are the connections for an "AT" style decoder with the sound connections on the back. This plug-and-play decoder is a drop-in replacement for the original circuit board on an HO F unit.

realistic sound, the speaker must have some form of enclosure or baffle. The enclosure keeps the air on one side of the speaker from getting to the other side. A speaker without an enclosure will sound distorted or tinny, and will be quiet.

The enclosure can be the locomotive body or tender shell, **6**. Most speaker suppliers also offer custom-made enclosures for their speakers. MRC, LokSound, and SoundTraxx supply enclosures with their sound decoders and speakers. Tony's Train Exchange has a line of precision speaker enclosures to fit its speakers, **7**. These plastic enclosures are custom-made to fit various sizes of speakers. Enclosures can be made from pill bottles or fabricated from plastic sheet, **8**.

Oval-shaped speakers are often the best choice if you have room to fit them, **9**. I installed a pair of oval speakers without a separate enclosure on the floor of an HO brass tender, **10**. The volume was low until I put the shell on. The volume then increased enough that I had to turn it down.

I have two F7 A-B sets with speakers installed. One non-powered F7B has two oval speakers installed in enclosures made from sheet lead soldered together. The other has two 1" round speakers in plastic snap-together baffles, **11**. The sound level from both is about the same, but because the oval speakers are larger, the sound of the diesel engine is a little deeper. The horn and other sounds are much the same. Remember the old saying about

stereo speakers: "The bigger the box, the better the bass."

Wiring a sound decoder in a diesel is pretty straightforward, **12**, but adding one to a steam locomotive means running multiple wires to the tender. The number of wires varies depending upon the location of the decoder or decoders, **13**. Micro connectors, such as those offered by Miniatronics, **14**, simplify these connections. My Daylight-painted 4-4-2 brass locomotive and tender needed a sound decoder. There was a problem because of the painted Vanderbilt tender. The solution was the small Tsunami decoder and small

speaker all installed in the engine. The only connection between the engine and tender is the drawbar, **15**.

Sound volume

One or two locomotives with sound at high volume may be OK, but get a bunch of them running at the same time, like at a club, and you have a discordant chorus.

Fortunately, most sound decoders have adjustable volume levels. The sound level is best adjusted so that you need to be near the engine to hear the sound. Individual sounds can be adjusted by changing the value of a

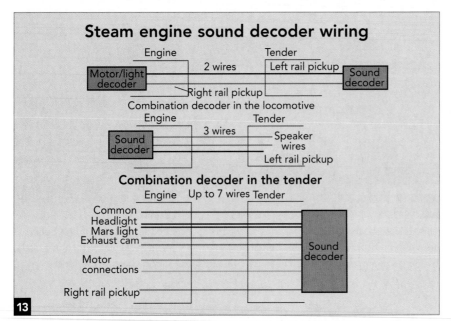

Steam engine sound decoder wiring

Engine | Tender
2 wires
Motor/light decoder — Left rail pickup — Sound decoder
Right rail pickup

Combination decoder in the locomotive

Engine | Tender
3 wires
Sound decoder — Speaker wires
Left rail pickup

Combination decoder in the tender

Engine | Up to 7 wires | Tender

Common
Headlight
Mars light
Exhaust cam
Motor connections
Right rail pickup
— Sound decoder

13

There are four approaches to installing a sound decoder in a steam engine. If you use two decoders, only two wires are needed between the engine and tender (only one if you use the drawbar as an electrical connection). With the decoder in the tender, all control wires must be connected to the tender. If you can squeeze the decoder in the engine, only three wires are needed (four if you add a backup light). If the decoder and speaker are all installed in the engine, only the drawbar connection is needed.

14

Micro connectors, available from Miniatronics, allow wires to run between the engine and tender. The white dots on the connectors show alignment. Two-, three-, and four-wire connectors are available.

15

The speaker, headlight, and decoder were all installed in this locomotive so the tender didn't have to be modified. A small speaker was installed under the stack.

CV. After testing on the programming track you can use on-the-fly programming to adjust sound levels. Check the manual for the CVs that control sound. If you're adjusting the sound on a split CV that controls two different sound levels, remember that you must write back both parts, all eight bits of the CV.

With LokSound, one press of F8 mutes the sound, just as with most other sound decoders. However, four levels of volume are also controlled with the F8 key: A double click of F8 increases volume. This happens four times, then the volume drops back to low and starts over.

Some decoders use a "magic wand" (a stick magnet) waved over part of the locomotive to change the volume.

Coordinating sound and light

Modern diesels use ditch lights that flash on approach to grade crossings. Key mapping allows you to turn on the horn and ditch lights at the same time. (See Chapter 5 for more on key mapping.)

You can also install two decoders in the same locomotive, one for better motor control and a second decoder for sound. As mentioned in Chapter 8, both decoders can be set to the same address. One of the decoders can be a function-only decoder.

Sound future

Advances in technology continue to put more memory on a chip, which has made possible 16-bit sound in a decoder that's smaller than the older 8-bit version it replaces.

Another growth area is custom sound files. There's no reason that new sound files can't be created and shared over the Internet. It would be convenient if a standard can be developed that will allow files to be shared among different brands of decoders and download adapters.

Ambient layout sounds (vehicle and industrial noises, for example) is another expanding area of the hobby. FantaSonics and Miller Models, among others, offer sounds that can be controlled using DCC decoders. The Dream Player by Pricom allows triggering of recorded sounds.

CHAPTER ELEVEN

Operating with DCC

It's no secret that Digital Command Control offers many operational advantages on large layouts, but—surprising to many—DCC is very useful on small single-operator layouts. The variety of DCC-equipped ready-to-run equipment gives us the time we once spent building rolling stock to have fun running trains. That, and the freedom from flipping block toggle switches, has generated more interest in layout operation following prototype practices.

Tom Towner brings a train into town using a wireless DCC throttle on his around-the-walls On3 layout. The railroad is patterned after California's Nevada County Narrow Gauge.

1

Turnouts can be thrown by hand on small DCC layouts or on those featuring walkaround operations.

2

Digital Command Control works well on author Don Fiehmann's small portable HO switching layout, which uses only a couple of locomotives. The Digitrax Zephyr or NCE PowerCab or Twin works well for this size layout. The turnouts are all within comfortable reach. The industries are cardboard cutouts from a catalog.

Layout variations

The ability to be closer to our trains lets us re-examine the old ways we operated a layout. The old ivory tower method of controlling trains from a central location is gone, as DCC—especially wireless—has made walkaround control standard.

Turnouts can be controlled remotely, or since operators are next to the trains they control, they can be operated manually. The dispatcher can also control turnout positions with a PC using a mouse. Smart phones and tablets have added the ability to operate trains and turnouts through Java Model Railroad Interface (JMRI; Chapter 12 goes into more details).

One of my first experiences with operation was on a 4 x 8-foot layout with enough tracks squeezed in to fill a garage. Turnouts were all thrown manually, and cars were uncoupled by hand, 1. This gave me the feeling that I was part of the train crew and not someone observing from the sidelines.

The ability to walk with your train has impacted the way larger layouts are designed. Digital Command Control has given a boost to linear, around-the-

wall designs and multi-level layouts.

All DCC systems have the ability to use walkaround cabs. Even the entry level Digitrax Zephyr Xtra or NCE Twin, with their all-in-one command station/cabs, allow handheld cabs to be connected.

Wireless operation has almost become the standard method to operate a layout. It gives more freedom to move and "flow" with a train without breaking concentration to find a plug for your cab.

Layout size doesn't matter

You can apply DCC to any layout in any scale. I have a 2 x 4-foot N scale layout that I use for DCC demonstrations. The layout includes all of the key DCC features, such as power districts, a reversing section, and decoder-controlled turnouts. It's small enough to be portable, with a handle that makes it portable. Two operators can use the layout with a Digitrax Zephyr and a UT-4 throttle or an NCE PowerCab and a Cab04 throttle.

I also have a small portable HO switching layout that's fun to operate, 2. The layout lets operators assemble or break down a local freight, and it's small enough that all the manual turnouts can be easily reached. Normally I run two locomotives: one to do the switching and a small road locomotive, like an F7, to pull the train.

On the other end of the spectrum are big layouts, like Dave Parks' large Cumberland and B&O home layout, 3, and the Silicon Valley Lines club layout in San Jose, Calif., 4. The Cumberland layout uses Digitrax and the Silicon Valley Lines uses an NCE system. Digital Command Control can be used to run trains by yourself as well as with multiple operators.

Digitrax ran a poll on its Website asking layout owners how many operators usually run trains at one time. A total of 61 percent reported that they usually run trains by themselves, 17 percent reporting just two operators, and 22 percent three or more.

My home layout encompasses an area the size of a two-car garage. Although up to five operators can run trains, most of the time it's just me.

Operating sessions on Dave Parks' large layout can use up to 20 operators. Dave's layout is really two different railroads in one layout. It's difficult to try and operate both of these at the same time due to the limited amount of aisle space around the layout. Only one of the railroads is operated at a time. The WM uses timetable-and-train order operations, and the B&O uses signaling.

Computer control

Most DCC systems utilize a serial port, USB connection, or other interface to connect the system to a computer. The computer need not be state-of-the-art, **5**. A used laptop can normally handle the job.

Hardware connections are made in different ways. For Digitrax systems, RR-Cirkits makes a USB-to-LocoNet adapter called the LocoBuffer-USB. NCE Power Pro systems use a serial (RS-232) connection to the command station, and NCE has a USB adapter planned for the PowerCab. A Keyspan 19HS adapter placed between the USB and RS-232 will work between the NCE and a USB port. Lenz systems use an LI-USB or LI101F-232 for its XpressNet. The new ESoC system by ESU uses an Ethernet connection.

Several manufacturers offer DCC-related computer software programs. Java Model Railroad Interface (JMRI) is popular—and free! It allows you to set up control panels that let you dispatch or operate a layout from the computer, **6**, even from a remote location. With an onboard TV camera, you can even watch the operation.

Block occupancy and turnout positions can be fed back to a computer, with the status of blocks and turnouts shown on the display. With DCC bidirectional communication, locomotive positions can also be shown.

A handy use of a computer is to program decoders. Decoder Pro, part of the JMRI program, is a Java-based program that runs on PCs or Macs and can be used to read and write information on decoders. The CV data from a decoder can be saved to a file and then used to refresh a decoder if it loses its information. Decoder Pro also

Dave Parks' large home layout, the Cumberland and B&O, uses a Digitrax system with wireless throttles. Up to 20 operators can run trains at one time. Bob Jacobsen and Dave are going over the evening's train schedules at left.

The Silicon Valley Lines is a large two-level club layout with a helix connecting the levels. The club uses an NCE DCC system with wireless cabs. Operators can use their cabs to operate turnouts as well as run trains.

allows having an on-screen throttle to run a locomotive with a mouse.

Another part of the JMRI program, Panel Pro, allows users to set up a Centralized Traffic Control (CTC)-type dispatcher's panel. Users can also create an on-screen control panel to operate turnouts controlled with accessory decoders, **7**.

CTC operation

The simplest way of modeling CTC (Centralized Traffic Control), where the dispatcher controls turnouts and signals to guide trains, is with a computer. The computer determines turnout positions by the DCC commands it sends to the layout. By adding block detectors that feed layout information back to the computer, you have all the data needed to set up a CTC panel. With bidirectional communications between the system and decoders, the computer knows which locomotives are in which blocks.

If operators control turnouts locally using conventional push-button or toggle switches, the computer won't know the turnouts' positions. This can be fixed by using accessory decoders with

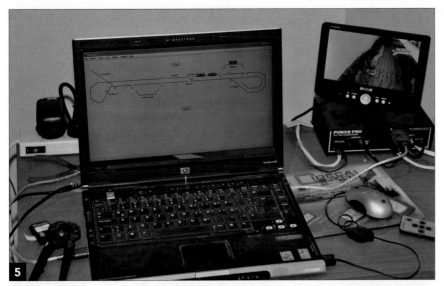

5

This simple dispatcher's setup in Buenos Aires, Argentina, features a laptop running Java Model Railroad Interface (JMRI). The video link at right allows a dispatcher to observe operations. *Adrian Pardo*

6

Jim Betz dispatches trains on the Cumberland and B&O layout using computerized controls with dual displays.

feedback capability or by using micro-switches on each switch machine.

The Silicon Valley Lines dispatcher currently uses a magnetic board to track train locations, **8**, but the club plans to interface both Macs and PCs to the Ethernet via a wi-fi connection. The Ethernet will feed a serial port adapter that interfaces to the DCC system. This will allow a dispatcher to control the layout from another room using a portable computer. The club plans to use Panel Pro for the CTC

panel and turnout control.

Layout operation with DCC is going on worldwide. Photo **9** shows Adrain Pardo communicating with other operators during a session in Buenos Aires, Argentina.

Automatic operation
Advancing technology allows packing more features into newer decoders. One example, asymmetric DCC, is part of the new Lenz Gold Series decoder. This decoder has the ability to

automatically stop at a station or signal, triggered by a section of track that automatically controls the train speed as it stops.

The braking functions are controlled by bits in CV51. The automatic stop can be directional, so trains are only affected while traveling in one direction.

Asymmetric DCC can be used to control a display layout or run trains in the background or on a second main line on a single-operator layout. This feature can be used in conjunction with the ABC (Automatic Brake Control) feature (see the next section) that sets a constant stopping distance regardless of speed.

This feature is activated by an offset in one of the phases of the DCC signal fed to the rails. Asymmetric DCC is triggered with a section of track fed by an uneven string of diodes, **10**. Having more diodes in one direction than the other makes the DCC signal uneven and triggers this feature. Engines without the asymmetric DCC feature (or those that have it turned off) are unaffected by the stopping section.

Automatic Brake Control
Another Lenz Gold Series decoder feature is Automatic Brake Control (ABC). This feature, which sets a constant stopping distance, is activated by setting bit 1 in CV51. The length of stop is controlled by the value in CV52.

I ran a test of this feature with a passenger train to see if the train would stop with the last car at the point where the brake was set (speed step 0). Once the value of CV52 was adjusted for the length of the train, it would stop from any speed when the engine passed a point and have the observation car stopped precisely where I set the speed to zero. At slower speeds, the train came to a gradual, prototypical stop. At the highest speed, the train would roll past the point where the brake was set, then stop rapidly. Once activated, the function continues until it's finished. The ABC feature can be used with Asymmetric DCC to make an accurate station stop automatically at any speed.

Rolling stock identification

Real railroads must keep track of the thousands of freight cars rolling across their rails. To do this, all cars are equipped with AEI (Automatic Equipment Identification) tags, small computer chips in plastic boxes mounted on the sides of cars. Trackside readers use passive radio signals to get information such as reporting marks, road number, and car type from the tags as cars roll past.

Doing the same thing on a model railroad may sound futuristic, but the Silicon Valley Lines club has been experimenting with a similar system based on radio frequency identification (RFID). The system uses the same small chips placed under the skin to identify pets. Special low-cost readers recover the information in the chips.

Since these chips are small and relatively inexpensive, one could be attached to the underside of each piece of rolling stock. Each chip would have an ID number that would relate to a database in the computer. This file would contain the reporting marks and road number of each car, and club layouts could add owner identification.

This would allow running a freight train into a yard and having a computer print out a list of cars in the train. Cars' destinations could also be in the database.

Sound ideas

The growing interest in locomotive sound is spilling over into other parts of the layout. Look for sound to become an even more important part of layout scenes. Several new items make sound even easier to use.

Model Rectifier Corp. makes a series of what it calls "sound stations" for producing layout sounds. The company makes units for depot and locomotive sounds.

SoundTraxx produces a system called SurroundSound. This system uses bidirectional communications to determine the location of an engine on the layout. The system then feeds layout-mounted speakers near the engine, allowing use of larger speakers to

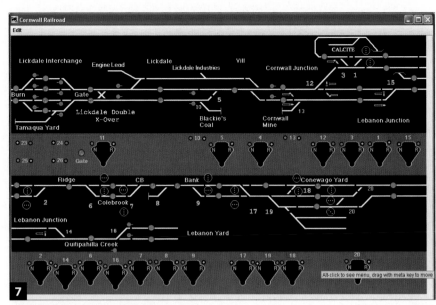

Nick Kulp built the main control panel for his Cornwall Railroad using JMRI Panel Pro.

Silicon Valley Lines dispatcher John Plocher tracks train movements using a magnetic board. The club plans to convert to computer displays for dispatching. John develops Arduino devices for DCC.

reproduce low-frequency sounds. Other background sounds can be integrated with the locomotive sounds.

Layout sounds

There's a growing interest in adding other types of sounds to a layout. Most layouts have some form of noise-producing industry, such as a saw mill or mine. How about the sound of running water and birds singing near a waterfall? Sounds like these should be kept at a low level, allowing them to be heard in the background when

you are near the source of the sound. A company that specializes in sounds for layouts is FantaSonics (www.fantasonics.com). A growing number of available sounds include waterfalls, stamp mills, lumber mills, and so on.

The Dream Player by Pricom Design (www.pricom.com) allows triggering of recorded sounds. Pricom has a series of Dream Players, **11**. These devices can be programmed to play back ambient sounds. They can be triggered by switches, block detectors, sensors, or your DCC system.

This is an operating session in Buenos Aires, Argentina. Adrain Pardo uses a headphone/mic for communications. *Adrian Pardo*

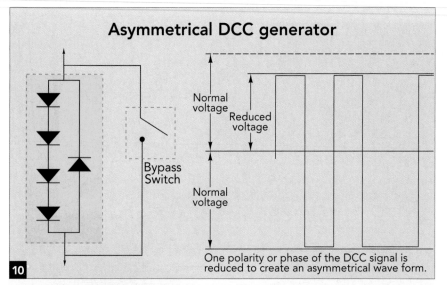

Asymmetrical DCC generator

Bypass Switch

Normal voltage

Reduced voltage

Normal voltage

One polarity or phase of the DCC signal is reduced to create an asymmetrical wave form.

The Dream Player by Pricom is designed to produce layout sounds. It uses a standard SD memory card, and can control up to four different sounds. It works well for adding ambient sound to a scene. Pricom has released a "Pro" version of the Dream Player with more functions.

Easier layout operation

Owners of standard DC layouts often have to spend a lot of time explaining their control systems for visiting operators. The many power assignment methods using toggle and rotary switches, as well as block boundaries, can easily confuse new operators.

With DCC, very little instruction is needed. Former *Railroad Model Craftsman* editor Bill Schaumburg, who in the course of his duties visits many layouts, commented to me that with a DCC layout, someone only has to put a cab in his hand and with little explanation he is off and running.

It's getting hard to find clubs that have not switched to DCC. They've realized the improvements DCC has to offer. I've heard of one club that had a

few diehard DC users who didn't want to convert to DCC. However, when these members had the chance to run a DCC layout without the hassle of electrical block switches, conversion plans to DCC started. (That club is now converted to DCC, but still can switch to DC.)

As technology advances, manufacturers continue to pack more features in smaller chips and at lower prices. More DCC-related products are appearing on the market, making DCC easier to install and more flexible to use. Super-capacitor module add-ons have all but eliminated locomotive stalling due to poor wheel/rail contact.

The shift in model railroading toward ready-to-run products allows more time to do railroading. This has generated an increased interest in prototypical operations, with more layouts now designed to host operating sessions. The NMRA's Operations Special Interest Group (Op SIG) offers a regular newsletter for modelers interested in realistic operations. The group's gatherings offer a chance to run various layouts and interact with other modelers sharing similar interests.

The future of DCC operations

Bidirectional communication, allowing the locomotive and the command station to exchange information, is on the horizon. Digitrax calls its system Transponding and Lenz calls its technology RailCom. The NMRA is looking at RailCom as a standard. This system will allow a computer to track locomotives' locations on the layout.

Also coming are decoders that simulate the use of fuel and water. They will stop a locomotive if it runs out of fuel or water, and the only way to reset ("refill") the tender or fuel tank is on special tracks in front of the water tower, coal dock, or engine servicing area. There are already CVs assigned for coal/fuel (CV894) and water (CV895).

Remote uncoupling is an item that you may see more of in the future.

Another possibility is a type of power limiter that senses drawbar pull, which could allow an engine to pull only its true tonnage rating.

CHAPTER TWELVE

DCC and today's technology

It's hard to find a modeler who doesn't have access to the Internet. The Internet, Wi-Fi, and DCC are all digital and function very well together. There are groups and forums for communications between modelers and manufacturers. You can even watch videos on subscription services like *Model Railroader* Video Plus to learn more about DCC.

The Internet and inexpensive laptop computers along with smartphones and tablets have opened up a whole new world of model railroading. This chapter will show the many ways the Internet is used in the hobby. *Adrian Pardo*

This is a novel way using an iPhone or tablet in video mode to take a ride on a layout. The resulting video will show you views you've never seen before. *Adrian Pardo*

A variety of DCC topics and videos of sound-equipped models can be viewed online at *Model Railroader's* website and its subscription service, *Model Railroader* Video Plus.

Your smartphone or tablet can operate a layout with Wi-Fi using Java Model Railroad Interface (JMRI), a free online program for programming decoders and operating your model railroad.

Ride the rails

An iPhone or other type of smartphone can be used to take a ride on the layout using the video mode, **1**. I found it very interesting when I installed a miniature video camera in one of my cabooses. It's amazing what you find in tunnels!

Searching for solutions

Search engines like Google, Yahoo!, and Bing make it possible to find information on almost any aspect of DCC. All it takes is a few key words to find a wealth of information on items like installing decoders, wiring, and lighting, among other topics.

If you can't find answers to your questions with search engines, you may want to check out the various Yahoo! Groups (www.groups.yahoo.com) that focus on DCC topics. These groups are made up of fellow modelers from around the world. With DCC, it's a pretty safe bet that someone else has had the same problem you do and has an answer.

There are Yahoo! Groups devoted to almost every DCC manufacturer. Other groups cover broader topics like layout sound and DCC wiring. Answers to questions often come from

somebody knowledgeable about the topic, and there will likely be multiple responses. Most groups have archives with a string of questions and answers that you can search by keyword. These groups are not help lines sponsored by a manufacturer with someone available 24/7, so it may take some time for someone to read your question and return with an answer. There is even an occasional bit of humor sprinkled in with the replies.

It's easy to search for the group or groups that you're interested in. Some groups need to approve new members. Responses from the group come as an e-mail. There are a few options on how you can receive the replies.

If you can't find a group you're interested in, you can create a new group. The groups can be open or closed. The latter lets you restrict membership to members of your club or other interested persons. I belong to a restricted group interested in DCC that meets once a week for lunch.

Video channels

Video is a great source of information. YouTube has a large number of videos on DCC and other model railroading topics, but the quality varies.

Model Railroader magazine has videos on its website, as well as its subscription service *Model Railroader* Video Plus, **2**. On these two sites, you can see and hear the latest sound-equipped locomotives and learn how to program decoders.

Java Model Railroad Interface (JMRI)

Java Model Railroad Interface was originated by a group of modelers in the Silicon Valley. They realized it would be a lot more convenient to be able to program and store decoder settings using the power of a computer. Java was selected because it will run on many different OS platforms. Java is available for Windows, Macintosh or Linux, and it works with a full range of DCC systems, including C/MRI, Digitrax, EasyDCC, Lenz, and NCE, among others.

JMRI is divided into three areas with different applications: DecoderPro for programming decoders; PanelPro for layout operation, signaling and control panels; and SoundPro for controlling layout sound and lighting.

Two program levels of JMRI are maintained: a test version and a release version. The test version is used for debugging newly added and modified software. When the test version works satisfactorily, it's elevated to the release version.

When new decoders are released, new definitions are needed. One of the JMRI contributors can volunteer to create the new software definition. The DecoderPro software is user-friendly because it uses names for the configuration variables and CV numbers, which are both displayed.

How we use DecoderPro is similar to how we use newer telephones. In the past, we used to remember

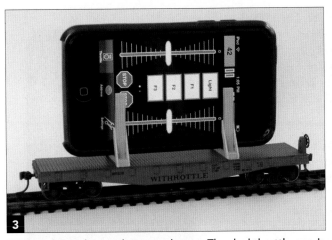

3

WiThrottle can be used to run a layout. The dual throttle app is shown. *B. Hoffman*

4

The new Tool Box app from Digitrax provides manuals, videos, and more. It's available for iOS and Android devices.

telephone numbers. Now we store names and the phone remembers the numbers. DecoderPro remembers the CV numbers and shows you the name of the function. This takes a lot of the mystery out of decoder programming.

Once you are satisfied with a decoder's settings, they can be saved in a roster file. Complete rosters of all your locomotives can be stored for future use, which is handy if you need to restore a decoder. A stored file can program a new decoder and then change the locomotive address.

An interesting ability of PanelPro is setting up remote wireless control panels on smartphones or tablets. Multiple panels can be accessed and toggled between using the tab function of the browser. Larger tablets work best in this application. Smartphones work better as cabs.

Another feature of JMRI is WiThrottle, **3**, which sets up a Wi-Fi link to smartphones and tablets. The app is designed for the iPad, iPhone, or iPod touch. WiThrottle Lite is free and will run one locomotive (address) at a time. It controls speed and emergency stop plus all 28 functions. An inexpensive version of this app will run two trains, do consisting, and set up routes through JMRI. It can be set up as a road or yard throttle.

WiThrottle is available from the Apple App Store. These devices work only with Apple's iOS system. The Wi-Fi connection doesn't need an Internet connection; it will operate with a router.

Visit WiThrottle's Website, www.withrottle.com, for more information.

There are a lot of help files on the JMRI website. There are also several YouTube videos that show setting up and operating JMRI.

Since JMRI is an open-source project, it's growing and evolving in many directions at once. If you're interested in getting involved in one of the many levels, check out the Website, jmri.sourceforge.net

Digitrax Tool Box

Digitrax has an app for iPad, iPhone (iOS), and Android devices called the Tool Box, **4**. This app is well done with lots of text, manuals, and how-to videos. There are even manuals for discontinued products available at this site. To get the app for either iOS or Android, go to www.digitrax.com and do a search for Tool Box.

Touchscreen Cabs

A smartphone or tablet is a powerful battery-powered handheld portable computer. They have the capability of being wireless cabs with a touchscreen. Recently, there's been a lot of activity in turning handheld smart devices into portable wireless cabs/throttles. There are many different ways that this can be accomplished. An operator can bring their smartphone or tablet from home to the club and use it as their cab for the operating session, then go home and use it there. The club could have a Digitrax system and the home an NCE system and

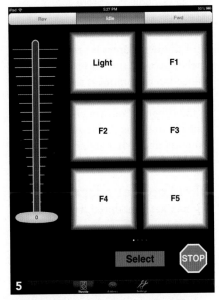

5

This screenshot taken on an iPad illustrates the controls for a locomotive. This is the standard version for locomotive controls.

the smart device would work for both through JMRI, **5**.

Wi-Fi on Android OS tablets and phones

Android is an operating system used in most of the new non-Apple tablets and smartphones, **6**. There is an app called Engine Driver that uses the same Wi-Fi connection to JMRI. This app will work with WiThrottle, allowing a mix of IOS and Android devices on the same JMRI system.

TouchCab

TouchCab, **7**, is an app that will work with an ECoS or Lenz command

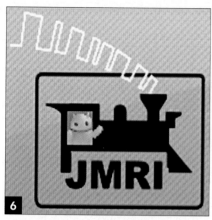

6

Engine Drive is an Android app that works with WiThrottle. Two versions are available, a free and a deluxe version from the Google Play Store.

station. The Lenz model 23151 USB and Ethernet adapter is attached to a wireless access point via an Ethernet connection or command station via XpressNet. The TouchCab app works on the iPhone/iPod. TouchCab is available from the Apple App Store. A computer and JMRI are not used with TouchCab.

Wi-Fi LocoNet adapter LNWI

Digitrax has announced its entry to the expanding Wi-Fi model railroad control market with a new adapter. This adapter forms a bridge between

Wi-Fi and the LocoNet. The LNWI doesn't need a PC or Mac. It uses an iPad or iPhone and other Smart Phone as a cab. Apps for the LNWI are coming to the Apple App Store. Check the Digitrax Website for more information.

Devices for layout control

There is a growing interest in controlling layout sounds, signaling, and lighting. One device that is getting a lot of attention is the Arduino, **8**. It's a low-cost, programmable, general-purpose microprocessor that comes on a circuit board. Plug-in attachments are available to make it easy to bread-board and connect to a USB port for programming. *Model Railroader* ran an article on operating turnouts with the Arduino in its June 2013 issue.

The Arduino code (C/C++) can be shared over the Internet. A good start for more information is an Internet search for "Arduino DCC." The voltage range is compatible with DCC.

Pricom has a new Layout Lighting Solutions system that can be set up with a computer to operate layout lighting. Check its Website (pricom. com) for more information.

The new AUX-BOX DCC is a stationary DCC decoder that can

7

TouchCab is an iPhone app for use with Lenz and ECoS systems using a Lenz 23151 adapter. *TouchCab*

control up to eight devices. The outputs are rated at 3 amps and are electrically isolated. Dave Parks uses the AUX-BOX to power the staging tracks on his layout (see Chapter 11), allowing power to be turned off when the block isn't used. This quiets idling sound locomotives.

NMRAnet

This network is in the development stage. The NMRAnet is an enhancement to DCC that allows distributing computing. One application would be for more-prototypical signaling, where each block could communicate with the next block. If you are interested, check the Internet for NMRAnet.

The future is here

Internet programs, apps, and handheld devices can be combined to run locomotives and control layouts, with more possibilities on the way. All this is possible through the open-ended applications of DCC. Modern technology is attracting a new, younger generation of enthusiasts to model railroading. The future is certainly bright for the hobby.

8

The Arduino is a small, low-cost microprocessor that can be programmed for DCC applications such as turnout control. Arduino circuit boards are also available in smaller sizes, the micro and the nano.

Glossary of DCC terms

Accessory (stationary) decoder – Decoder used to control trackside devices such as turnouts, signals, and lights.

Address – The value programmed into a decoder so it will recognize and respond to the correct command sent from the command station. A decoder can have more than one address, but will only respond to one address for direction and speed depending on the mode of operation.

Amp (ampere) – The basic unit of electrical current.

ASTRAC – Analog command control system built by General Electric in the mid-1960s.

Automatic reversing unit – A booster or adapter that detects a short as a train enters or leaves a reversing track section. When the short is detected, the unit reverses the polarity of the power to the loop to clear the short.

Back-EMF (back-electromotive-force control) – The voltage developed by a motor when it is rotating. Used by some decoders to stabilize motor speed.

Bipolar – A signal that goes from plus to minus and returns, without stopping at 0 volts. This is the type of wave form that DCC puts on the rails.

Binary – A number system using only digits 0 and 1.

Bit – The smallest element of the DCC signal. A bit is either a 0 or 1.

Byte – Equals 8 bits or 2 nibbles. A configuration variable (CV) is one byte.

Booster (power booster) – A device that combines power from a transformer and the data from the command station and feeds it to the rails.

Booster district – The wiring from the booster to the circuit breaker. Connects to the power district.

Broadcast packet – A special packet that will be acted on by all decoders that receive it. Used in service-mode programming on the program track, and also used as an emergency stop for the entire layout.

Cab (throttle) – Device that originates commands to locomotive and stationary decoders. Can be handheld and either tethered or wireless. Communicates with command station over a bus or network.

Cab bus – Wires or cables connecting the cabs (throttles) to the command station.

Circuit breaker – A device used to shut off power to a section of track when an overload or short circuit occurs.

Command station – The brains of the DCC system. The command station receives instructions from a cab and converts them to command packets that are fed to the booster(s).

Common rail wiring – Wiring style where one rail is continuous, providing a common return for power; the other rail is divided into blocks, districts, or subdistricts. Not commonly used for DCC.

Control bus – Wires or cables that run from the command station to the booster(s).

Consisting – Controlling more than one locomotive as a single unit. In basic consisting, all decoders in a consist have the same address. In universal consisting, the command station sends each locomotive in the consist a command. In advanced consisting, the decoder knows it's in a consist and responds to a consist address command used by all units in a lashup.

Configuration variables (CVs) – The memory locations in a decoder that are changed during programming.

Digital Command Control (DCC) – Method of controlling trains by using digital communication packets to send commands over a common network.

Decimal – Numbering system based on digits 0 to 9.

Decoder – A device that receives DCC commands and controls motors, lamps, sound, and other functions. Can be either mobile or stationary.

District – A section of the layout powered by a single booster.

Fast clock – A clock that runs at a fast rate to compress time. Fast time can be adjusted from 1:2 to more than 1:20. Often used for timetable operations.

Function key mapping – The ability to map which function key on the cab controls which output in the decoder.

Function output – The output(s) from a decoder designed to operate lamps, light-emitting diodes, and other on/off devices.

Hexadecimal (HEX) – Numbering system that uses digits 0 to 15 (digits 10 to 15 are represented by letters A to F).

Ground – The common, or return, path in an electrical circuit.

Interoperability – The National Model Railroad Association's standards and recommended practices allow a decoder from one manufacturer to operate with the command station/booster of another manufacturer.

Interrupt – Communication between the cab and command station where the cab "interrupts" the command station when it has a command to send. See "polling."

Keep-Alive – The trade name of TCS decoders equipped with a super-capacitor module. The capacitor allows the decoder to operate with a momentary disruption in power, such as that caused by dirty track.

Light-emitting diode (LED) – Used for signals and locomotive lighting. LEDs are long lasting, draw little power, and run cooler than incandescent bulbs.

Lighting – Most decoders have output functions for lights. Some can drive special effects such as Mars (moving) lights, strobes, and firebox flicker.

Macro – A group of instructions or commands that requires only a single keystroke. Used to set up routes through multiple turnouts.

Microcontroller – Miniature computer on a single chip that has outputs and memory for a self-contained program and configuration variables. Used in decoders.

Microprocessor – Miniature computer on a single chip. Memory and output are on separate chips.

Momentum – Electronically adding the effects of weight and speed to a train or locomotive. Controlled by CV3 and CV4.

Nesting – Combining methods of consisting into a single-unit consist. All are controlled by a single command.

Nibble – Equal to 4 bits or half a byte.

National Model Railroad Association (NMRA). – Establishes standards and recommended practices for Digital Command Control.

Occupancy detector – A device that detects the presence of a locomotive in a section of track.

Ohm – Unit of resistance to the flow of electricity. Resistors are rated in ohms.

Operational (ops) mode programming – Programming a locomotive's decoder on a non-programming track. Also called programming on the main.

Packet – A single DCC command comprising a preamble, address, instruction, and error byte.

Polling – Communications system between the cab and command station where the command station continuously asks each cab in sequence for its information.

Power bus – Wires that carry the power/signal from the booster to the rails.

Power district – An electrically isolated portion of a layout connected to its own booster. Since it's separated from other power districts and boosters, short circuits will not shut the entire layout down.

Power supply – The source of electricity that feeds the command station and booster(s).

Programming – The process of changing the values in a decoder's CVs.

Programming track – An isolated section of track used to program decoders.

Protocol – Format of the signals sent between units. The DCC protocol is defined by NMRA standard 9.2.

Return – Name for the common, or ground, path in a circuit.

Reverse loop – A section of track where the train can reverse its direction of travel. By doing so, the difference in the polarity on the rails at some point will cause a short circuit. See "automatic reversing unit."

Read-only memory (ROM) – Memory that can't be changed by programming.

Route – A group of turnouts and their specified positions triggered by the activation of a single "TOP" switch address to a specified position. (Digitrax)

Service mode programming – Used on the programming track to set up and read decoders. Uses broadcast packets to address any decoder regardless of its programmed address.

Stiction – The friction that causes a surface to stick when stationary then attempt to move.

Speed stabilization – Feature of some decoders that use the back-electromotive force of a motor to level out the speed of the motor under changing loads.

Speed table – A table in the decoder that controls the relationship between the speed step command and the actual speed of the motor.

Sound decoder – A decoder that produces diesel, steam, or electric locomotive sounds. Combination motor/sound as well as sound-only decoders are available.

Stall current – The number of amps drawn by a motor when power is applied and the motor is held and not turning. Normally tested at 12 volts.

Snubber – A resistor capacitor network used at the end of a long cable run. This is used to compensate for some of the inductance accumulated in a long cable run.

Super capacitor – A capacitor with up to 10,000 times more capacity than an electrolytic capacitor.

Tethered – Cabs or throttles connected to the system through a cable or cord.

Transponder – A device that acknowledges the receipt of a message. Used in some newer decoders to let the command station know that they have received a command. Also used to communicate the location of a decoder on a layout. (Also see "bidirectional communication.")

Two-rail (house-type) wiring – Wiring style where two wires are run from the power source to the device it feeds; two wires are run from the booster to the rails. The most common DCC wiring. (See common rail wiring.)

Volt – The "pressure" of electrical power. Standard DCC has 14.25 volts on the rails.

Watt – Measurement of electrical power. Calculated by multiplying volts and amps (14.25 volts x 0.5 amps equals 7.125 watts).

Wi-Fi – A wireless digital method of communications for a small area like a home. Normally connected to a modem or gateway for access to the Internet.

Wire – Size is measured by gauge: The larger the number the smaller (in diameter) the wire. The electrical resistance of wire is proportional to its cross section; heavier wire has a higher current capacity.

Wireless cab – A cab that uses either radio waves or infrared light to communicate with the command station.

Troubleshooting techniques and hints

Over the years, other modelers and I have developed a number of techniques and hints for locating and fixing Digital Command Control problems. Some of these may sound obvious, but it's amazing how often they are overlooked.

• The first thing to look for is something simple. Is it plugged in?
• If the trouble isn't where you're looking, it must be someplace else. Did someone turn the power switch off at the wall?
• Check in the last area you or somebody else worked. Did somebody drive a staple through the scenery and into the wiring?
• Divide and conquer. Start in the middle and then determine which side the problem is on.
• Test each stage of wiring as you work on it. It's better to work in small sections and discover problems than finish an entire layout to find something is wrong.
• Easter egging: Start changing parts until you find the bad one.
• Even though a wire connection may look good, it may not be solid electrically. A cold solder joint or wrong IDC (insulation-displacement connector) is a good example.
• If it has a battery, swap it for a fresh one or charge it.
• If something isn't working and the voltage is OK, check the common return on that device.
• If all else fails, read the manual. Can't find the manual? Check the Internet for a replacement copy.
• Talk your problem over with someone else. Even if they aren't knowledgeable about the subject, just talking about it can help your thinking process.
• Check user groups on the Internet to see if somebody else had the same problem. The answer to your problem may only be an online search away.
• Once the trouble is found, the problem often is very obvious—that is, once you found it.

DCC manufacturers and suppliers

Manufacturers

Accu-Lites Inc.
118 S. Main St.
Wauconda, IL 60084
www.acculites.com

Bachmann
1400 E. Erie Ave.
Philadelphia, PA 19124
www.bachmanntrains.com

CTI Electronics
P. O. Box 9535
Baltimore, MD 21237

CVP Products
P.O. Box 835772
Richardson, TX 75083
www.cvpusa.com

DCC Specialties
57 River Rd., Ste. 1023
Essex Junction, VT 05452
www.dccspecialties.com

Digitrax
2443 Transmitter Rd.
Panama City, FL 32404
www.digitrax.com

Fantasonics Engineering
695 Crescent Ave.
Orcutt, CA 93455
www.fantasonics.com

Iowa Scaled Engineering
12395 Gull Ln.
Peyton, CO 80831
www.iascaled.com

Innovative Train Technology Products
P.O. Box 5042
West Hills, CA 91308
www.ittproducts.com

Lenz USA
c/o American Hobby Distributors
57 River Rd., Ste. 1023
Essex Junction, VT 05452
www.lenzusa.com

Loksound
477 Knopp Dr.
Muncy, PA 17756
www.esu.eu/en/start/

MTH Electric Trains
7020 Columbia Gateway Dr.
Columbia, MD 21046
www.mthHOtrains.com

Model Rectifier Corp.
80 Newfield Ave.
Edison, NJ 08837
www.modelrectifier.com

NCE
82 E. Main St.
Webster, NY 14580
www.ncedcc.com

Pricom Designs
www.pricom.com

Protocraft
www.protocraft.com

QSI Solutions
P. O. Box 967
Colchester, VT 05446
www.qsisolutions.com

Richmond Controls
P. O. Box 1467
Richmond, TX 77406
www.richmondcontrols.com

SoundTraxx
210 Rock Point Dr.
Durango, CO 81301
www.soundtraxx.com

Sprog DCC
www.sprog.us.com

Team Digital
www.teamdigital1.com

Train Control Systems (TCS)
P. O. Box 341
Blooming Glen, PA 18911
www.tcsdcc.com

Suppliers

All Electronics Corp.
14928 Oxnard St.
Van Nuys, CA 91411

Aztec Manufacturing Co.
2701 Conestoga Dr., Unit 113
Carson City, NV 89706
www.aztectrains.com

Decoder Installation Services
3721 O'Henry Dr.
Garland, TX 75042
www.dccplus.com

Evan Designs
1140 U.S. Hwy 287
Ste. 400-225
Broomfield, CO 80020
www.modeltrainsoftware.com

Litchfield Station LLC
1412 N. Central Ave., Ste. D
Avondale, AZ 85323
www.litchfieldstation.com

Micro-Mark
340 Snyder Ave.
Berkeley Heights, NJ 07922
www.micromark.com

Miniatronics
561-K Acorn St.
Deer Park, NY 11729
www.miniatronics.com

Ngineering
www.ngineering.com

SBS4DCC
8229 Euliss Ct.
Avon, IN 46123
www.sbs4dcc.com

Steve's Depot
P. O. Box 816
Burlington, MA 01803
www.stevesdepot.com

Tan Valley Depot
www.tamvalleydepot.com

Tony's Train Exchange
Pinewood Plaza
57 River Rd., Ste. 1023
Essex Junction, VT 05452
www.tonystrains.com

TVW Miniatures
www.tvwminiatures.com

Ulrich Models
566 E. 16th Ave.
Longmont, CO 80504
www.ulrichmodels.biz

Acknowledgements

DCC continues to improve. No one person knows all of the ins and outs of DCC. Some of these friends helped me with the original edition of *The DCC Guide* and have continued adding their expertise to this second edition. Great thanks go especially to Howard McKinney, Mark Gurries, Frank Geraci, Adrian Pardo, Tony Parisi, Vince Vargus, Jim Betz and my wife, Marla. Without their support this second edition would not have been possible. — *Don Fiehmann*

About the author

As an IBM electrical engineer (he holds a patent relating to reading magnetic strips on credit cards), Don Fiehmann has been able to apply his electronics expertise to model railroading for more than 50 years. A life member of the National Model Railroad Association, Don got his start with model trains with a Lionel set in 1947. His interest in model railroading was renewed with the birth of his son, Brent, in 1964. This led to developing a number of electronic throttles, including the SST-7 and SWAC-2, published in the 1970s. In 1976 he designed and published the first article on direct radio control for model locomotives.

Don has written more than 60 articles and reviews in the modeling press. His first book was *Basic Electricity and Electronics for Model Railroaders*, published by Kalmbach in 1988. This was followed by the first edition of *The DCC Guide* in 2008.